Heritage, HIGHBALLS, and Hijinks

Heritage, HIGHBALLS, and Hijinks

Colorful Characters I Have Known

Ridley Wills II

Ridley Wills II

Printed in the United States of America

14   13   12   11   10   1   2   3   4   5

ISBN: 978-1-4507-1421-7

Cover design by Joey McNair

Page design by Holly Jones

*This book is dedicated
to all those Nashvillians
who have the courage
to be nonconformists.*

Contents

Acknowledgments

Because of concern that such a personal book as *Heritage, Highballs, and Hijinks: Colorful Characters I Have Known* might cause some consternation among the families of the people about whom I've written, I decided to share my manuscript with either close friends or family members of each one.

———◦◦◦◦———

So much has been written about Minnie Pearl's extraordinary life that finding material on her was easy. *Minnie Pearl, An Autobiography* was particularly helpful. I also shared my manuscript with Minnie Pearl's niece, Lillias Burns, who reassured me that I had made no major errors.

———◦◦◦◦———

I interviewed Neil Cargile Jr.'s first wife, Connie Stevens Kelly, about the years she and Neil were married. That was a pleasure as Connie was completely open with me. I also gave Allen Cargile a copy of the manuscript on his older brother. Allen was helpful, both in his comments and in lending me three photographs. As so many Nashvillians did, I read John Berendt's colorful article on Neil, which appeared in *The New Yorker* magazine in January 1995. Many of the cross-dressing episodes I wrote about came from that rich source.

———◦◦◦◦———

In the summers, Irene and I spend much of June and July at the Monteagle Sunday School Assembly, which is only seven miles from the DuPont Library at the University of the South. While at the assembly in 2009, I spent a considerable amount of time in the DuPont Library archives looking through the thick files on Dudley Clark Fort, Andrew Lytle, and Frederick Tupper Saussy III. Dudley's son, Arthur G. Fort, a longtime friend, was kind enough to read my manuscript on his father. I appreciated his interest in doing so.

⸺⸻◦◦◦⸻⸺

Nobody helped me more with the chapter on Mildred Gulbenk than her daughter, Anne Cowan Cain, who graciously shared so many stories of a mother she dearly loved. Mildred's second husband, Roupen Gulbenk, was also generous with his time, providing me with stories of the thirteen years he and Mildred shared in marriage. He also lent me two good photographs of Mildred. Eugenia Moore was also particularly helpful. Her late husband, Ben Moore, and Mildred were first cousins. Eugenia shared some wonderful stories about the many times she, Ben, and Mildred were together.

⸺⸻◦◦◦⸻⸺

Haun Saussy, Tupper's gifted son, who is a well-respected professor at Yale, read what I wrote about his father and shared some of his rich childhood memories. Tupper's sister-in-law, Jeanie Hecker Cammack, also read what I had to say about Tupper, and corrected several mistakes.

⸺⸻◦◦◦⸻⸺

I got to know Betsy Howe because we were both charter members of The Downtown Presbyterian Church when it was founded in 1955. I recall and admire her dedicated efforts to ensure that this national landmark was not torn down. Others who helped me with stories about Betsy were her first cousin once removed, Harry Howe Ransom; her nephew, Robert L. Howe; Dr. Frederick T. Billings III;

her next-door neighbors, George C. and Ophelia Paine; and her friend, Ann Street. I still wish Ann had told to me the name of the other couple at Betsy's house, Washington Hall, the memorable night Betsy threw the dinner party for the New York art dealer.

I knew Andrew Lytle because, for many years, my family enjoyed using the Weaver cottage, which was next door to Mr. Lytle's, at the Monteagle Sunday School Assembly. Everyone at the Assembly who knew Mr. Lytle respected him and enjoyed his wit and wisdom. I appreciate Brad Gioia sharing with me his memories of Andrew Lytle's kindnesses to him when Brad was an English major at the University of the South. Brad also read my manuscript on this Agrarian giant. Andrew's daughter, Pamela, also read the manuscript and corrected several mistakes. It was nice to reconnect with Pamela who knew my wife, Irene, when they were children at the Monteagle Sunday School Assembly.

Researching Dan May's extraordinarily productive and colorful life was made easy because his son Jack, a good friend, shared so generously with material on his father. I still am grateful for the relatively unknown role Dan May played in bringing Metropolitan Government to Nashville and Davidson County.

Missy Pride Edwards was married to Lewis Pride, Harvey Pride's younger brother, until Lewis' untimely death. Missy read my manuscript on Harvey, whom she knew well. Her sons, Dan and Eugene Pride, spent part of the Fourth of July weekend with me at Missy's Monteagle cottage last summer, sharing their memories of their Uncle Harvey. My cousin Trilby Elliston Williams was very interested in reading what I had to say about Harvey. She was one of his dearest friends. Phillys Scruggs, who, with her husband Julian were in Harvey's tight circle of close friends, also read my manuscript on him. Phillys lent me a wonderful photograph of Harvey going over a jump at a Hillsboro Hounds event. My friend Eugenia Moore read my script on Harvey and added her stories to the mix.

<hr>

It was wonderful that Ellen Stokes More Wemyss's son, Livingfield More Jr., took such an interest in my project. He went over my manuscript on his mother with a fine-toothed comb more than once, and corrected errors I simply missed. His daughter Ellen also read the manuscript. I'm grateful to Ellen because she put me in touch with Sid Waits, a Covington County, Alabama, historian, who filled me in with information on the nine years Ellen and her first husband, E. Livingfield More, lived in River Falls, Alabama. Fletch Coke, a former regent of the Ladies' Hermitage Association, worked closely with Ellen Wemyss when they served together on the LHA board. Fletch and her husband Bill both shared interesting stories about "Miss Ellen."

<hr>

Late in her long and fruitful life, Margaret Lindsley Warden wrote her autobiography, *Life Has Been Very Kind to Me,* which I thoroughly enjoyed. Margaret and I were fellow members of The Downtown Presbyterian Church for more than half a century. We shared interests in genealogy, the Belle Meade Plantation, and preservation. With my memories and by referencing her book, writing about this remarkable woman was both fun and easy.

<hr>

In writing about Margaret Wyatt, I was helped immeasurably by referring to *Nothing Happens By Chance*, the book she wrote about her own life. Margaret was first cousin of Granbery Jackson Jr., my wife's father, and we spent much time with her. In addition, Margaret's niece, Kay Russell Beasley, who was wonderful to Margaret during her later years and who assisted Margaret in producing her autobiography, was an enormous help by carefully and skillfully editing what I wrote to ensure that it was factually and grammatically correct.

———≈◦◦◦≈———

I am grateful to everyone else who helped me, including my wife Irene and our good friend Ann Wells. I relied on their sound judgment and suggestions. Irene also carefully read my manuscript in April 2010 and made a number of constructive changes. Thank you, Irene. Finally, I am indebted to Fiona Soltes, Holly Jones, and Joey McNair whose skills as a copy editor, book designer, and cover designer, respectively, have helped me enormously. For anyone who has plans to write a book, I want to emphasize how important it is to have highy skilled professionals assist you in editing and design.

Chapter 1

By Way Of Explanation

Perhaps a friend stated it best: "We do seem a hotbed for odd sorts here." She mentioned it offhand in regards to a single subject of this book, but her words ring true. Nashville and its environs have indeed been home to a great many colorful characters and truly unique individuals, many of whom I've called friends.

As a local historian, I've taken great delight in learning more of their stories and delivering them here for future generations—not to mention sharing the tales for our own good memories, too. Besides, having recently completed *The Hermitage at One Hundred: Nashville's First Million Dollar Hotel*, I decided I needed a change of pace in my writing career.

Currently, I am heavily involved in writing the history of the YMCA of Middle Tennessee for a comprehensive book on this outstanding institution. Over the years, I've written ten other books—biographies of prominent Nashvillians, histories of several Middle Tennessee families, stories about the lives of Tennessee governors, a book highlighting my Tennessee postcard collection, a shorter history of the YMCA of Middle Tennessee, and histories of the Belle Meade Country Club and Montgomery Bell Academy. While researching and writing all these books has given me much pleasure, I thought it would be great fun to share a number of profiles of the standout characters I have personally known. My wife Irene told me it was fine to do so, but that I should put it aside when I finish and let one of our sons publish it after my death. I disregarded this good advice simply because I want to enjoy reminiscing about these people with friends who choose to read what I've put on paper. And here we are.

All the people included are Southerners, and all lived at least portions of their lives in or within ninety miles of Nashville. Like most Southern cities, Nashville offers a treasure trove of interesting citizens. Note that those presented here are in alphabetical order, rather than simply placing the most colorful first. Included in this book are stories about Sarah Ophelia Cannon, better known as Minnie Pearl; Neil Cargile Jr., who was both a fabulous and fearless pilot and a cross-dresser; "Uncle" Dudley Fort, the most interesting member of a family loaded with interesting people; Mildred Joy Gulbenk, who believed in the spirit world and was a minister in the Catholic Apostolic Church of Antioch; Elizabeth "Betsy" Howe, who was both good and outrageous; Andrew Lytle, the Agrarian writer and editor of the *Sewanee Review*; Dan May, who presided over Nashville Rotary Club meetings in tennis shoes and kept Nashville's Metropolitan Government alive by steadying Beverly Briley when he seemed to falter; Harvey Pride Jr., whom everybody loved and whose favorite expression was "Oh, Gawd"; Tupper Saussy Jr., the most sophisticated and charming ex-convict I've ever known; Margaret Lindsley Warden, who wrote a Horse Sense column for *The Tennessean* for fifty-five years, and who lived in the same house next door to Ward-Belmont College (later Belmont University) from 1913 until 1988; Ellen Stokes More Wemyss of Gallatin, Tennessee, who lived to be one hundred and six and who continued to ride her horse until she was ninety-two; and Margaret Early (Mrs. Hubert) Wyatt, of Franklin, who was the most Unreconstructed Rebel I've ever known.

I considered writing about a number of other unique Tennesseans, including Edward H. "Boss" Crump, whom I always enjoyed reading about when I was growing up, and whom I once saw outside the Hermitage Hotel leaning on his walking cane. I decided to leave him for the Memphians.

In the 1960s, Nashville had two inner-city politicians of a lesser stripe, Gene "Little Evil" Jacobs and Henry "Good Jelly" Jones. Little Evil fought Metropolitan Government tirelessly. In the weeks preceding the Metro election, he had placards made that read "Russia Has One Government" and another that read, "Castro Has Metro." Little Evil, who wore a trademark white hat, hung around the courthouse and the police station on a daily basis, and was popular in his Second Ward. Good Jelly Jones, an African-American, owned a North Nashville restaurant that was often called "a bootleg joint" and a "good-time house." He carried carloads of North Nashville voters to vote against the 1962 charter election. The stories were legendary, but not knowing either gentleman personally, I felt they didn't qualify for my first team.

During high school at Montgomery Bell Academy, I would sometimes attend basketball games at Father Ryan's gymnasium on Elliston Place. There were two things unusual about that place in the late 1940s and early 1950s. One, it had a parquet floor. The other was that, at halftime, "Black Cat" Riley would sweep the floor and shoot baskets underhand from center court. Occasionally, he made one. Black Cat, a huge sports fan, was also a fixture selling newspapers on the streets downtown. Alas, Black Cat and I never met, even at Al's Tavern (now Rotier's Restaurant for you newcomers).

There have been plenty of intriguing golfers at the Belle Meade Country Club, as well. One was Mack Brothers, who took advantage of a crooked arm to entice unsuspecting golfers at various country clubs across the South to play him and his cohort, Dudley Casey, for money. Willie Gibbons, the now retired Belle Meade Country Club golf pro, got several long-distance phone calls from Mack and Dudley's angry victims.

I considered putting Capitol Hill reporter Drue Smith in my book. Drue was Chattanooga's gift to Nashville. All the politicians and lobbyists on Capitol Hill knew and liked this outgoing lady, known as the "media queen" of the city. I also gave thought to including my friend, Jim "Iron Man" Pickett, a Nashville real estate man who loved bird hunting and who claimed to be a great athlete at Vanderbilt University. He told me he was better than John N. "Bull" Brown, Vanderbilt's All-American guard on the 1926 football team. He also said that, as a teenager, he once swam down the Cumberland River from his home in Neely's Bend to the foot of Broadway, then ran the nearly two miles out to Vanderbilt. In 1990, when Jim was nearly ninety, he came close to shooting my friend, Ernest "Willie" Hardison III, on opening day of dove season. It happened at Meeting of the Waters, the farm Irene and I had just bought and one where Iron Man thought he had exclusive dove-hunting rights. Only when Willie told Jim that his father was Ernest Hardison, a successful businessman who won the 1944 Iroquois Steeplechase on the horse Bank Robber, did Mr. Pickett put down his shotgun.

Someone who came closer to making the cut was James Hanner Armistead Jr. a great practical joker and friend with a quick wit. Early in his National Life and Accident Insurance Company career, Jimmy and his wife Betty lived in New Orleans, where Jimmy sold debit insurance door to door. Jimmy and Betty often came home for weekends, staying with her parents, Mr. and Mrs. Runcie Clements Jr., on Clarendon Avenue. While in the Clements' house on one such weekend, Jimmy shot himself in the foot with a shotgun. His friends said that he would do anything to get off the debit and come back to the home office. I question that.

Another time, in 1968, Jimmy was invited to ride the construction elevator that scaled the outside of the still-incomplete thirty-one-story NLT tower. The next day, I asked him if the ride scared him. He quipped, "Yes, but it didn't take me long to go home and change clothes." Once, while living on Chickering Road, Jimmy and Betty came home from a party at Bebe and Marcus Harton's house where they enjoyed after-dinner drinks of coffee, coffee ice cream, and Jack Daniels mixed in a blender and served in Champaign glasses. Jimmy's reflexes were sufficiently impaired that, when he drove into his garage, he did not apply his brakes soon enough and hit the wall between the garage and his den, buckling it. The next morning, Mrs. Clements came by and noticed the bulge in the den wall. She asked her daughter Betty, "Are you remodeling?" For years, Jimmy played practical jokes on Bernice Miller Denton. It never seemed to work, as Bernice's retribution was invariably worse than whatever Jimmy did. Maybe Bernice should have been the one in this book.

I really wanted to include John Jay Hooker. I showed him what I'd written about his amazing and productive life. Upon reflection, he felt my description of the conditions that caused Minnie Pearl

Fried Chicken to fail was incorrect. Perhaps he was right. As it is easier to write about people who are no longer living than to write about friends still alive, it seemed best to leave him out. So, I ended up with the six men and six ladies I mentioned earlier, all colorful and all interesting. I hope no one gets upset with what I've written and, conversely, that everyone enjoys the stories I've put on paper. I realize that, over time, stories sometimes become exaggerated, and that may well have happened with some of the ones in this book.

Regardless, these stories were too good not to share. Let the history lessons begin.

Chapter 2

Sarah Ophelia Colley Cannon
1912–1996

Consider the word "character," and there sits Minnie Pearl. There was just something about her; the way she grinned, the way she delivered a joke, the way she gave a welcoming "How-DEE!" every time she took the stage during her fifty-year career made you feel like you knew her, whether or not you actually did.

Most Nashvillians would be quick to claim Minnie Pearl—born Sarah Ophelia Colley on October 25, 1912—as their own. Though she came into the world in Centerville, right next to a tiny, unincorporated community called Grinder's Switch that would later play into her Grand Ole Opry fame, Sarah certainly left a mark in our capital city, and on many individuals, as well—including myself.

It was back in the 1970s when my cousin Laura Ragland McKay and her husband moved to Nashville. Mel McKay was a Harvard University English major who had decided to drop out of school to write country music songs. I helped Laura get a job as a programmer at National Life and Accident Insurance Company. My mother, Ellen B. Wills, also wanted to help, so she called Sarah and said, "Sarah, this is Ellen Wills and I'm calling because my great niece and my great nephew-in-law are here from Boston. He wants to make it in the country music business as a songwriter." My mother, who had gone to Ward-Belmont College just like Sarah, mentioned to the Grand Ole Opry star that she would love for the relatives to see her house. Sarah lived next door to the house where my Wills grandparents lived, a home that is now the governor's mansion.

Gracious as could be, Sarah told my mother she would love to meet the McKays. She had a funeral to go to but would come by the Wills home on the way to the funeral. So she arrived about eleven o'clock that morning, and sat on the couch in the living room between Laura and Mel. They had a nice visit and sipped apple juice that my mother had served. They never did get to see Sarah's house, but later, thanks to Sarah's introductions, Mel got to showcase his songs at some recording studios. Unfortunately, everything went downhill from there as the record producers told Mel, a New Englander, that his lyrics were a little complicated. After working in a warehouse for a number of months, Mel decided to return to Harvard, where he got his degree. He went on to become a private school headmaster.

Sarah crossed paths with our family again when my wife Irene was chairman of the Swan Ball. More on that in a moment. In the meantime, some history is in order.

Sarah was the youngest of five daughters of Fannie Tate House and Thomas K. "Tom" Colley. A native of Franklin, Tennessee, he was a prosperous lumberman who owned a sawmill in Centerville. Mrs. Colley was a college graduate, an accomplished pianist and a member of a respected family that had lived in Franklin for generations.[1]

Ophelia, as she was called, grew up with the whole town of Centerville as her playground. The only place she could not go was to the riverbank for fear that she might drown. As a child who never learned to swim, she feared only two things: the Duck River, which frequently flooded her father's sawmill, and rattlesnakes. Although she was the youngest member of her class, Ophelia graduated from Hickman County Grammar School as valedictorian. She then attended Hickman County High School, where she was an enthusiastic cheerleader who often shouted herself hoarse. Interested in dramatics, she took "expression" and enjoyed acting in school plays, including one put on by the Wayne P. Sewell Production Company of Atlanta, Georgia. Ophelia thought the director, a young lady in her twenties, had the most glamorous job in the world.[2]

When Ophelia entered her senior year at Hickman County High School in 1929, she dreamed of going to study at the American Academy of Dramatic Arts or the Pasadena Playhouse. The stock market crash ended those possibilities, as her daddy's business was hard-hit. Instead, Mr. Colley told Ophelia she could go either to the University of Tennessee for four years or to Ward-Belmont College, a prestigious two-year finishing school in Nashville. Because Miss Inez Shipp, Ophelia's expression teacher in high school, told her that Ward-Belmont had an exceptionally good drama department, Ophelia chose to go there. She had not been at Ward-Belmont twenty-four hours when she realized she was out of her league. The school smelled of "old money" and Ophelia felt immediately out of place in the midst of sophisticated, wealthy girls from Nashville, Dallas and Atlanta. Her ability to play the piano saved the day, as three upperclassmen, "Hot," "Dot," and "Annie," thought her piano skills were great and took her under their wings.[3] After finally getting in the swing of things, Ophelia began to enjoy herself. She majored in theater, took dancing, and became involved in all sorts of extracurricular activities. When Ophelia, whom her father called "Phel," graduated in the spring of 1932, she was not the same girl who had entered Ward-Belmont two years earlier. No one cried harder than Ophelia did when she and her classmates stood on the steps of Academic Hall and sang their alma mater, "The Bells of Ward-Belmont."[4]

After graduation, Ophelia opened a little studio in her home-town of Centerville where she taught dramatics, piano, and dancing. Having been changed by her college experience, however, she felt like she was in prison. In August 1934, Ophelia obtained her first theatrical job with the Wayne P. Sewell Production Company, the touring company she had been exposed to when she was in high school. Her responsibility was to produce and direct plays and musicals for local organizations in small towns across the Southeast. The towns soon became a blur, but Ophelia was gaining confidence in her ability to pull a cast together "in a ridiculously short time." While producing a play in Baileyton, Alabama, in January 1936, Ophelia stayed for ten days in the log cabin home of a mountain family, whose dialect and mannerisms she decided to copy. To complete the hillbilly image, she also began referring to herself as "Cousin Minnie Pearl."[5] After she left the little village fifteen miles from Cullman for her next assignment, Ophelia stopped by Centerville and told her parents about her visit with the mountain family, imitating the old lady as she talked. Mrs. Colley said, "Why Ophelia, you sound just like an old mountain woman! You always were a mimic!" Mr. Colley then said, "You'll make a fortune off that someday, Phel, if you keep it kind." What a prophetic comment.[6]

Ophelia first used her Cousin Minnie Pearl stage name while putting on a production for the Sewell Company in Aiken, South Carolina, in 1939. She would leave the company the following spring after six strenuous years on the road. The coming of radios, recordings and even movie theaters to rural areas had removed the need for a company like Sewell. Depressed that the experience had not catapulted her to "the glamorous world of Broadway," Ophelia returned to Centerville where Bob Turner, a Nashville banker, saw her perform at a small bankers' convention. Impressed, he told Harry Stone, then general manager of WSM-AM radio, that she was good enough to be on the Grand Ole Opry. Stone called Ophelia and invited her to an audition in Nashville. Ophelia, who was then running a Works Progress Administration recreation program for children in Centerville, said, "I couldn't get there fast enough." Having passed the audition, Ophelia was invited to appear on the Opry for the first time on November 30, 1940. Although she was scared to death, her debut was so successful that she was invited to return, starting a relationship with WSM that lasted fifty years.[7]

In the 1940s, one of Ophelia's closest friends was Orra Williams, a young woman from Fayetteville who was secretary to Jack Stapp, program director at WSM. Orra and Ophelia roomed together in a large boarding house on West End across from the Vanderbilt University gym. Orra wrote some of Minnie's comic material. Other material came from Minnie's early experiences in Centerville, and from her sister, Virginia, who wrote most of Ophelia's script for the first three years she was on the Opry.[8] Friends from Centerville realized that some of her characters were drawn from Centerville natives.

Minnie Pearl began to appear on stage in simple dresses with puffed sleeves, to wear a dime-store straw hat with a price tag hanging from it, and one-strap Mary Jane shoes. She also began to perfect her delivery. She would invariably open her act with that previously mentioned "How-DEE!" followed by, "I'm jes' so proud to be here!" One of her consistent and most popular monologues had to do with her dimwitted yet wise kinfolk, "Uncle Nabob" and "Brother," a character based on the tall, shy son of the mountain lady Ophelia had stayed with in Baileytown, Alabama. One of Minnie Pearl's favorite Uncle Nabob stories follows.

"The first car came through Grinder's Switch on a hot summer morning when Aunt Ambrosy was sitting on the front porch shelling peas. She heard the noise, then looked up and saw this thing coming at her. She jumped up, flinging peas everywhere, and ran into the house hollering for Uncle Nabob. 'Come quick,' she screamed. 'There's a varmit—biggest one I ever saw—just a'roaring down the road.' Uncle Nabob went running out on the porch with his shotgun and fired at the automobile. It terrified the man driving, who jumped out and ran for the woods. When Aunt Ambrosy heard the shot she called out from her hiding place in the parlor, 'Did ya kill it?' 'Naw,' Uncle Nabob answered. 'But I made it turn that fellow a' loose.'"[9]

Then there was the story about the first train to come through Grinder's Switch. Uncle Nabob saw it and said, "If that thing ever comes through here sideways it'ud wipe us plum off the map."[10]

During the 1940s, Orra and Ophelia would come for Sunday dinner at the home of Orra's cousin, Judith Ann Carter "Hez" Andrews, who lived on Warner Place in Belle Meade with her husband Jim and their two sons, David and Nelson. After starving all week, the young women were thrilled to have a good meal. When Hank Williams moved to Nashville, Minnie Pearl befriended him. Several times, she and Orra brought him to the Andrews' on Sunday. Hez's son Nelson sized him up. Nelson later wrote that Williams "could be the most charming of men or as morose as a funeral dirge. I later concluded that it all depended on his relationship with drugs on a given Sunday." In later years, Sarah, as she was known in Nashville, was most gracious in helping Nelson on various civic projects, particularly ones having to do with the Salvation Army and the American Red Cross.[11]

Orra Williams loved arranging dates for Ophelia. After Orra married Bill Pitner in 1946, she and Bill became insistent that Ophelia, who was then thirty-four, meet Henry Cannon, whom Bill had grown up with in Franklin, Tennessee. At that time, Ophelia was focused on being on the road all week performing across the South and Midwest and coming home each weekend for her Grand Ole Opry performances, where she was already popular and well known. She did agree to see him on the weekend and the meeting was, for Henry, love at first sight. As for Ophelia, she was swept off her feet. In 1947, Ophelia Colley married the handsome and witty Henry, who was a partner in an air charter service and a former Army Air Corps pilot during World War II. Orra was her matron of honor.[12]

Following their marriage, Henry set up his own air charter service for country music stars. Some of his clients were, in addition to Minnie, Eddy Arnold, Colonel Tom Parker, Webb Pierce, Elvis Presley, Carl Smith and Hank Williams. Henry was a cousin of Sam M. Fleming Jr., the longtime president and CEO of Nashville's Third National Bank and a descendent of Governor Newton Cannon. He and Sarah had no children, but enjoyed a great life together.

In addition to being an increasingly popular character on the Saturday night Grand Ole Opry, Sarah portrayed Minnie for many years on ABC TV's *Ozark Jubilee*. Later, she appeared with Junior Samples and others on CBS TV's popular and longstanding *Hee Haw* program. Her final network show was Ralph Emery's *Nashville Now* country music talk show on the Nashville Network cable channel.[13]

In 1957, Ralph Edwards' television show, *This Is Your Life*, was one of the most popular in the country. That same year, Sarah was asked to go to Hollywood to do some promotional film clips for NBC, commemorating WSM's twentieth year with the network. She had no idea this was a hoax to get her to Hollywood. Henry flew her to Hollywood in his Beechcraft. Thinking she was going to the NBC studios in Burbank for the filming, Sarah soon found herself in a dressing room with Claude Thompson, the best makeup man in Hollywood, having her eyes done. As she sat there, Sarah heard her mother's voice say, "Daughter, where are you?" Sarah came out of her chair like a shot, thinking she was either hallucinating or she had died and her mother was calling her. Then, she heard Ralph Edwards' voice say, "Sarah Ophelia Colley Cannon, this is your life!" Sarah grabbed her face and started crying. She turned around and

Minnie Pearl. "Hey Minnie, you're wanted in the kitchen!" From the postcard collection of Ridley Wills II.

there were her mother and her four sisters: Frances, Virginia, Mary, and Dixie. She pulled herself together and had a great time. Being on a Top Ten show opened new vistas for Sarah. In the next few years, she would do a lot of appearances on network television.[14]

In the 1960s, Nashville entrepreneur and two-time gubernatorial candidate John Jay Hooker Jr. persuaded Minnie Pearl to lend her name to a national chain of fried chicken outlets that would, he was convinced, successfully compete with Kentucky Fried Chicken. After starting off like gangbusters with the publicly traded stock having, at its zenith, a value of $64 million, people realized that the chicken wasn't that good and the venture collapsed amid allegations of accounting irregularities and stock price manipulation. The company, John Jay, his brother Henry, and Sarah Cannon were cleared of any wrongdoing. The negative publicity hurt, but fortunately, the sterling reputation of Sarah Cannon—and Minnie Pearl—remained intact.

By then, Sarah, as Minnie Pearl, was a country music legend, having won the hearts of Grand Ole Opry fans across the world. In 1965, she was named Nashville's "Woman of the Year." The next year, she became the first woman to be selected as *Billboard's* "Man of the Year" in country music. She was inducted into the Country Music Hall of Fame in 1975 and into the Comedy Hall of Fame in 1994. In 1992, she was awarded the National Medal of Arts.[15]

In 1969, Sarah and Henry bought that large home on South Curtiswood Lane that my mother wanted the McKays to see. They were wonderful neighbors to a succession of governors and were frequently guests at the executive residence to entertain or be entertained. Frank Clement was a huge country music fan and a close friend of Henry and Sarah. Later, when Winfield Dunn was governor, Sarah and Henry came to a country supper at the executive residence with Winfield and his wife Betty, Mr. and Mrs. Buddy Killen, and movie star Burt Reynolds. They played tennis, watched an NFL game on television, and sang "old country songs," led by Sarah at the piano. Reynolds was so taken by the evening that he later hosted a two-hour national television show from the executive residence on NBC.[16]

On another occasion, Betty Dunn invited a group of children from an Easter Seals camp to come to the executive residence. The children, wide-eyed with excitement, asked if they might meet Minnie Pearl, having been told she lived next door. Betty whispered to a state trooper to call Sarah to see if she might possibly come over for a few minutes. The First Lady of Country Music happened to be at home. She accepted, and in a few minutes she arrived to greet the children. They were sitting on the grass, standing on crutches, or in their wheelchairs under a tent in the front yard, enjoying juice and cookies. Betty Dunn remembers well what happened next: "After entertaining them for a few minutes with funny stories about Grinder's Switch, Mrs. Cannon asked the children to give her a gift. A look of wonderment came over their faces. She said that she knew they had been to camp and had learned some songs, and would they share some of them with us? Needless to say, they proudly sang their little hearts out, happily knowing that they had given something of themselves to Minnie and me."[17]

Tourists in buses and automobiles have traditionally ridden slowly down South Curtiswood Lane to take photographs of the Tennessee Executive Residence. Although they are not supposed to stop, some do. One day, when a tour bus stopped near the front entrance and people got out for a better look, Henry Cannon happened to be planting a bush in his front yard nearby. A lady walked over and asked him, "Do you work here?" Henry, who was wearing overalls, said he did. She then asked how long he had worked there. Henry deadpanned, "As long as Minnie Pearl has lived here." Not satisfied, the lady next asked if he was well paid. Henry replied, "No, but, if I do a good job, she lets me sleep with her." The lady turned on her heel and climbed back on the bus.

Now, as for that Swan Ball story. It was 1982, and Irene had spent several months unsuccessfully trying to land a known entertainer to

Sarah Cannon with her terrier, Heidi, 1981. Photo courtesy of Grand Ole Opry: WSM Picture—History Book.

perform at the swiftly approaching white-tie charity event. It was now February, and Irene called Sarah to ask her for ideas. They talked about the band Alabama, but Sarah thought they were a little rough. She then said, "I think Loretta Lynn would do a great job," and promised to have Loretta's manager call Irene. He did; Loretta and her manager agreed she would perform, although she was already booked that evening at the Grand Ole Opry. The plan was for her to drive to Cheekwood Botanical Garden, the site of the ball, immediately after her 9 PM Opry performance. The manager had just one request: He had to have a front-row seat, because Loretta was shy and would get upset if she could not easily see him when she came onstage. This was the first time the Swan Ball ever had a country music star perform. The performance was well received, and Irene was relieved and grateful to Loretta for coming and to Sarah for getting her out of a jam.

In her private life, Sarah loved playing tennis with good friends in the Charlotte-Pearl Tennis Group. Some of those who played with her in this group for many years were Ruthelia Buchi, Jean Clippard, Jo Doubleday, and Betty Dunn. One day when Sarah and Jo were driving to Franklin for a tennis game, a black cat darted across Hillsboro Road just in front of their car. Sarah slammed on the brakes of her blue Continental car and wheeled to the right shoulder of the road. Before Jo knew what was happening, Sarah was out of the car and in the middle of the highway. Jo watched her scratch the letter X in the pavement, and then spit on it. Almost as quickly, she got back in the car and said, "That will take care of that cat."[18]

One day Mary Ann Denney filled in for one of the Charlotte-Pearl regulars and was teamed up in a doubles game with Sarah. A scorcher was served just inside the center line. Sarah never even swung. Instead, she said to Mary Ann, "That thing went by me faster than salt goes through a widow woman!" Mary Ann was laughing so hard that she was ineffective for the rest of the set.[19]

Henry and Sarah Cannon were good friends of Governor Ned Ray McWherter, with whom they often had dinner. Later in her life, the governor would sometimes drop by her house in the afternoon for a drink. On his arrival, Sarah was apt to ask Henry to fix them "a little toddy," usually of Maker's Mark bourbon. With a wink, Sarah would say, "Of course, we don't drink before five o'clock, but it has to be five o'clock somewhere." On such occasions, the governor enjoyed hearing the Cannons' stories about Hank Williams and the Grand Ole Opry.[20]

Sarah was also an avid bridge player who participated in the same foursome each week. Every summer, the group would spend a week at the Monteagle Sunday School Assembly playing bridge. Two members, Sarah and Kathryn Whitehead, were very reluctant to leave their husbands, Henry Cannon and Frank Whitehead, alone overnight. Consequently, they would commute to Monteagle from Nashville every day in Kathryn's car. The ninety-mile trip took longer than one would expect whenever Kathryn stopped for gas. People at the service station would recognize Sarah and want to talk or ask her for an autograph. Always considerate of her fans, Sarah invariably complied.[21]

Eventually, however, the life caught up with her; she had a stroke. She had been playing bridge a few days before, interrupted several times by phone calls from her agent, continuing to ask about various appearances. Kathryn, realizing how much pressure was on her friend, said, "You must slow down. This pace is going to kill you." A few nights later, Henry heard her fall in her bathroom. He wanted to immediately call for an ambulance but Sarah told him not to because an ambulance would disturb their neighbors. Reluctantly, Henry agreed to wait until morning. He went into the bedroom, picked up two pillows and a blanket, and they lay side-by-side on the bathroom floor until daybreak, when he called 911.[22]

Later Sarah went to live in a nursing home, and in the first year of his administration, Governor Don Sundquist and his wife Martha paid a visit to her there. At some point, Governor Sundquist, who truly enjoys a joke, started to tell one. Sarah raised her hand and said, "Stop, stop right there! I don't meddle in politics, and you don't meddle in comedy."[23] Her fabulous sense of humor remained to the end.

Before she became ill, some of Sarah's favorite charities were the Humane Association, the American Heart Association, the American Cancer Society, and the Vanderbilt Children's Hospital, where she so enjoyed walking the wards and entertaining the children, whom she found to be precious and grateful for attention.[24]

After Sarah was diagnosed with breast cancer in 1985, she underwent a double mastectomy and chemotherapy at Centennial Medical Center. During her illness, she wanted to find a way to help others with the disease. So, in 1991, she lent her stage name to The Minnie Pearl Cancer Foundation and became an advocate for cancer education and research. Sarah Cannon died in Nashville on March 4, 1996, in her eighty-fourth year. Her life is so adequately summed up on her foundation's website. In addition to being a gracious individual, she was truly "a testament that laughter and a strong human spirit can bring joy to the world."[25]

Chapter 3

Neil Cargile Jr.
1928–1995

Deople saw Neil Cargile Jr. a great many ways. For me, though, an enduring vision was the very first one. I was a junior or senior at Montgomery Bell Academy back then, and there he was at a sorority dance, jitterbugging with one of the cutest girls. He was six or seven years older than she was, and had already been in the Navy as a fighter pilot. For teenagers in the early 1950s, that age discrepancy was huge. Everybody in the ballroom—particularly the girls—was aware of his presence.

The truth is, however, that Neil was rather known for being noticed.

Neil was born May 21, 1928, the oldest son of Eleanor and Neil Cargile, who owned Allen Manufacturing Company. The Cargiles lived on Lynnwood Boulevard when Neil and his younger brother Allen were youngsters. Ed Nelson, a friend and classmate of Allen in Parmer School, would sometimes spend the night with Allen. Ed's memory is that, when they were young, Neil was determined to win a local radio station's contest, the prize for which was a Piper airplane.

By 1937, the Cargiles had moved to a large home in the Jocelyn Hollow section of West Meade. There, at age twelve, Neil set up a machine shop in his parents' garage and built motor scooters out of washing machine engines. As a young teenager, he and a friend founded the Southern Maintenance Company, a clinic for putting ailing motor scooters and cars back in running order. Still later, he would transfer his mechanical skills to airplanes.[1]

Allen Cargile remembered in 1996 that Neil "once swapped a 22 rifle for a car. Here he was, fifteen years old, doing business with people twice his age. Before long, he had a 1927 Marmon, an eight-cylinder Cadillac and a sixteen-cylinder Cadillac. These older folk admired his initiative, but never thought he'd get those old wrecks, some of which had been in barns for years, running. He fooled them."[2]

Neil attended Montgomery Bell Academy his eighth grade and freshman years. In his sophomore year (1943-44), Neil attended McCallie School in Chattanooga and, as a junior (1944-45), he went to The Taft School, a preparatory school in Waterford, Connecticut, founded in 1890. He returned to MBA for his senior year, graduating in 1946. During one or more summers when he was in high school, Neil attended Culver Military Academy's popular summer camp with his brother Allen, Buzz Davis and Bill Cammack from Florence, Alabama.

In his profile in the *The Bell*, the editor wrote about Neil, "One of the most air-minded boys in school, Neil spends most of his time working with and talking about airplanes. He does, however, find time for football." Ronald Voss, Bob Coleman, Julian Scruggs and Vaden Lackey were some of Neil's closest friends at MBA.

At age sixteen, Neil built an airplane out of surplus parts of a World War II plane. He flew it solo from a field west of his parents' house that had 2200 feet for landing and takeoff. Neil became licensed to fly his plane when he was seventeen. His license did not allow him, however, to carry other passengers. Nevertheless, one day Neil called his friend Hamilton Wallace and told him that if he'd meet at H. G. Hill Jr.'s pasture, he would give him a ride in his plane. Hamilton, Jake Wallace, and Allen Cargile drove over to the Hill property. Soon, Neil's plane was spotted coming in for a landing. He stopped and Hamilton happily climbed aboard. Neil then taxied down the pasture but was unable to gain enough speed to take off. Jake and Allen watched Neil turn the plane around and come back for a second try. This time, the plane became airborne but did not gain enough altitude to clear the tree line. The plane crashed in the trees, losing a wing. Jake and Allen ran down the field to see if Neil and Hamilton were hurt. They were fine, but Neil was frantically hollering for everyone to leave as, having wrecked his plane, he had to report it to the Federal Aviation Administration and did not want anyone else to know that, when he crashed, he had a passenger.[3]

A daredevil pilot from the get-go, Neil soon flew loop-the-loops and once buzzed his father on the Belle Meade Country Club golf course. Mr. Cargile, who had been Vanderbilt's football captain in 1926, promptly grounded Neil for two months. Nashville newspapers properly called the younger Cargile a "backyard aviator." Neil had so many emergency landings that he also earned the nickname "Crash Cargile."

When John Seigenthaler was a senior at Father Ryan High School, he played linebacker on the Fighting Irish football team. In the game with Ryan's rival MBA, Bill Wade, a sophomore tailback, was already a star. Leo Long, who knew that, even then, Billy could throw the ball a mile, instructed John to tackle MBA's end, Neil Cargile, on every play. John did so, incurring at least one fifteen-yard penalty. However, Bill Wade was prevented from throwing to Cargile, and Ryan won the game fourteen to six. Years later, when Neil saw Seigenthaler, he recalled the dirty trick and called John a "son-of-a-bitch."

In the fall of 1947, Neil traded a motor scooter for a Fairchild PT-23. This was only one of a series of horse trades Neil did to acquire planes. Julian Scruggs Jr. remembered that, when Neil was a teenager, he owned and flew a Stearman PT-17. This may have been the same two-seater biplane that Jake Wallace remembered. Neil acquired the PT-17 by swapping the owner a 1929 Packard that Neil had been given by a family friend, and had put in running condition. He flew the Stearman PT-17 as far as Texas. On that trip, Mr. Cargile rode with him. Mrs. Cargile also had enough confidence in Neil's piloting skills to occasionally fly with him.[4]

Neil and Allen both had a fondness for speed. Brownlee Currey Jr. remembered in 2009 seeing Allen driving down Highway 100 at a high rate of speed with Neil hanging over the hood adjusting the carburetor. On another occasion, when Neil finished building his plane, he got an experienced pilot to give it a test ride. Brownlee

Currey Jr. said that, on taking off from a field, the plane barely cleared the tree line. Years later, Neil offered Tommy Trabue Jr., a ride in his powerful racing car up Nine Mile Hill. Tommy climbed in behind Neil, and off they went like a streak of lightning. Tommy claimed the car reached one hundred and twenty miles an hour, but admitted his vision was impaired because of the tight quarters. Tommy also remembered that Neil raced Ferraris in competition across the Southeast and Midwest, and nearly always won.[5]

Neil entered Vanderbilt University in the fall of 1946 as a freshman in the School of Engineering. His plan was to become an aeronautical engineer. That fall, he played on the Vanderbilt freshman football team and lived at home as Vanderbilt, with limited housing, did not provide dormitory space for in-town students. Later in the school year, Neil roomed with Julian Scruggs at the Sigma Alpha Epsilon fraternity house. On weekends, when he wasn't playing football, he usually was working on a plane in his parents' yard. However, he often drove to Jackson, Tennessee, where he kept several crop-dusting planes in a hangar at McKellar Field, an unused commercial airport that Neil leased for one dollar a year. He was earning extra spending money by spraying cotton fields in the Jackson area, and elsewhere. Once, Neil and three other pilots, including then-MBA student Franklin "Frank" Jarman, flew four Stearman PT-17s to Pine Bluff, Arkansas, to spray some cotton fields. This was not Neil's usual territory and some competitors in that part of Arkansas took exception to his presence. They ignited all four planes after dousing their tails with gasoline and destroyed them.[6] Neil decided to get the hell out of Dodge.

On another occasion, Neil was crop dusting with Frank Jarman and a couple of other guys in Madison County, Tennessee. This particular time, they were loading the Steadman sprayers at McKellar Field with a poison, using a pump. When the pump malfunctioned, Neil grabbed a garden hose to siphon the poison. To start the liquid flowing, he sucked on the end of the rubber hose, casually spitting out the small amount of poison that got in his mouth. With that task completed, he and his crew went to a "meat-and-three" restaurant in Jackson to eat. There, in the midst of lunch, Neil suddenly grew rigid and fell to the floor unconscious. His buddies revived him by throwing cold water on his face. Instead of going to a hospital, they finished lunch and drove back to the hangar. Neil said he was fine, and they picked up where they left off that morning.[7]

One day in the spring of 1948, when Neil, covered with grease, was kneeling in his parents' garage beside a half-dozen airplane cylinders, his mother called, "Do you have my flower bucket out there?" Neil said, "Yes, I've got it, but I'm using it. It's full of gasoline." At the time Mrs. Cargile asked about her flower bucket, Neil had three planes on the lawn, and airplane parts in the garage. Mr. Cargile made Neil move the parts out of the garage each afternoon before he got home from work so he could park there.[8]

In addition to being a fearless and skilled pilot, Neil was an accomplished dancer. During the winter social period, when he was in Vanderbilt and for years—possibly decades—to come, he attended high school fraternity and sorority dances at the Belle Meade Country Club. And just as I remember him, Neil and his date would often do the jitterbug surrounded by a ring of admiring friends.[9]

Also while at Vanderbilt, Neil met an attractive co-ed named Sue Nolte. Their romance was the talk of the campus. Later, in the fall of 1948, Mary Ann Stallings of Humboldt, Tennessee, transferred to Vanderbilt in her junior year, having spent her first two years at Huntingdon College in Montgomery, Alabama. Neil happened to see her on campus and asked her for a date the first night she was in Nashville. Mary Ann remembered in 2009 that he took her to the "Copia," a nightclub in the split of Highways 100 and 70. Neil dated her that fall. She found him to be attractive and a gentleman.[10]

Neil left Vanderbilt after his sophomore year to join the U.S. Navy, where he became an excellent pilot, stationed at the Pensacola Naval Air Station, home of the legendary Blue Angels.

Returning to Nashville after his discharge from the Navy, Neil reentered Vanderbilt, graduating in 1954 with a degree in mechanical engineering.[11] During all this time, he continued to work as a crop duster, piloting his own plane and hiring others to fly planes he owned. Sometimes, he worked the cotton fields in the Sikeston, Missouri, area. Once, while flying dangerously low over a cotton field in the Missouri Delta, Neil hit a metal stake that knocked off a tire. Realizing that he could not land on one front tire and the small one in the tail, he deliberately hit the stake two more times to dislodge his other front tire. When he accomplished this on the

Neil Cargile Jr. in the cockpit of his Navy fighter November 11, 1951.
Photo courtesy of the Nashville Public Library, Special Collections.

second try, he then skidded to a rough landing on the plane's belly. Understandably, Neil became an area legend.

A much more prevalent danger to crop dusters like Neil, however, was power lines. He told his pilots that, if you see you are going to hit a power line, you should "jam the rudder real hard. That way, your propeller will cut the lines and you won't get hung up." Neil also told them that, if they were going to crash, to pull themselves into the middle of the plane by grabbing the control stick and the plane would "ball up" around them; when it stopped rolling, they could get out and climb into another plane. His advice probably saved some lives, including that of Frank Jarman.[12]

On another occasion, Neil was in Courtland, Alabama, trying to lease an unused Air Force base there. For some reason, he didn't have a way back to Nashville. Realizing that his friend John Bransford Jr. was flying somewhere near Louisville, Kentucky, Neil called a Nashville air controller and asked him to track down John. Soon, John got the radio request for a ride home for Neil. He told the air controller, "Tell Neil I'll pick him up in about an hour."[13]

<hr />

Bloomfield Hills, Michigan, is about as different from Courtland, Alabama, as you can get. Neil once had an attractive girlfriend who lived in that affluent Detroit suburb. As her parents had a big back-yard, she agreed for Neil to have four huge containers containing four small planes shipped there. Neil had bought the planes sight unseen. Sometime after he and Frank Jarman uncrated the plane parts, Neil realized that they would have to cannibalize one to end up with three complete planes. Once they assembled the planes, Frank looked around and asked Neil how they were going to get them out of the yard. The nearest place they could take off was from a field on the other side of a creek that ran by the yard. Neil said, "Watch this." He then taxied each plane up to the creek and, in succession, "walked" each one across the creek to the field.

In the early 1950s, Neil began dating Connie Stevens, a high school tennis star who, after graduation from Harpeth Hall, went to Briarcliffe Manor Junior College in New York. In April 1955, while Connie was still in her second year at Briarcliffe, she and Neil, who was seven years older, married. Connie would have preferred waiting until that summer, when she would have graduated, but Neil was insistent that they go ahead. Because Briarcliffe did not promote tennis, a sport she loved, and school was not academically challenging, Connie went along with Neil's wishes. After their wedding, a lovely reception at the Belle Meade Country Club, and their honeymoon, Neil and Connie moved to Sikeston where he remained in the crop-dusting business. Living in the small southeast Missouri town was a culture shock to Connie, whose exposure beyond Belle Meade was an exclusive finishing school for young ladies.[14] Because she was so unhappy in Sikeston, they returned to Nashville after a few months. Back home, Neil worked briefly for Mr. Stevens, but that didn't last long. Neil was not cut out to work for anyone else. He tried unsuccessfully to convince Mr. Stevens to back him in the boat-building business. Mr. Stevens wisely declined. Once, while vacationing with Bob and Ann Coleman in Florida, Neil disappeared. He told Connie that he was investigating the possibility of going into the dredging business.

Neil continued to pursue his passion for flying while married to Connie. One day, when they were young adults, Neil flew Ed Nelson, Valere Potter, and his brother Allen from Berry Field to Indianapolis, where they visited a friend of Valere's. Neil's father drove some of the group to the airport. Just as the prop plane was ready to take off, with Neil at the controls, he casually told his friends to break out the chewing gum. Neil, having noticed a slight leak in the gas tank, chewed his gum for a minute or two then stuck the wad on the tank to plug the leak. His companions did likewise. With that taken care of, they took off. Before they got to their designated cruising level, the control tower instructed Neil to return to the Nashville airport. Neil said, "Oh, shit," thinking that a mechanic had noticed the leak. When they landed, an employee met Neil and said he had mistakenly taken his father's car keys, and that Mr. Cargile was pretty hot. Neil tossed them out of the window and flew to Indianapolis.[15]

In 1956, Connie had a baby boy, whom they named Neil Cargile III. Five years later, Connie gave birth to a little girl, whom she and Neil named Cornelia. They called her "Lia." The next year, 1962, Connie and Neil divorced.

After that, the dredging idea resurfaced. Neil became engaged in designing, building, and operating mammoth dredges that were used to deepen river channels and harbors and to find gold and silver, often in remote parts of the world.[16] His close friends were under the impression he made a great deal of money in the dredging business, only to lose it and then turn around and make it all over again. Part of the problem is that his lifestyle was very expensive, as were the airplanes he continually purchased, flew and maintained. One of the many planes he owned was a Piper J3C-65 fixed wing single engine manufactured in 1946.

Neil's second wife's name was Tommie. He called her "Tommie Tomato." They had a son named Hastings. That marriage, however, also failed.

Neil Cargile Jr. standing beside his plane in front of Nashville Flying service hanger, circa 1955. Photo courtesy of Allen Cargile.

In about 1970 or 1971, Neil joined the Nashville Polo Club even though he was not an experienced rider. He got by through athleticism and toughness. Neil, however, was different from the other polo players. Often, he would forget to bring some needed item, such as a saddle. At one point, he modified a school bus to haul his horses around. His greatest contributions came when he would host visiting polo clubs on his boat on Old Hickory Lake. He would do this the evening before matches, keeping the opposing team on the lake until late at night and supplying them—but not himself—with plenty of liquor. The next day, still feeling the ill effects from their late-night sojourn with Neil, the visitors often fell victim to the Nashville Polo Squad even when the visitors had superior horses and a better team. Willie Hardison remembers Neil buzzing the polo field in Edwin Warner Park in a jet.[17]

In 1970, Lucy Roberts, a daughter of Jack and Anne Byrn Roberts of Lebanon, Tennessee, told her parents that a friend of theirs had asked her for a date. When asked who he was, Lucy said "Neil Cargile." At first her father thought she meant Neil Cargile III. Anne Byrn immediately realized that Lucy was talking about Jack's SAE fraternity brother at Vanderbilt Neil Cargile Jr. Anne told her husband, who then went ballistic. Needless to say, Lucy Roberts never went out with Neil Cargile Jr. [18]

⸻∘⚬∘⸻

Neil's reputation preceded him, especially when it came to wearing women's clothes. The first time Neil ever wore women's clothes in public may have been at a Halloween party at the Palm Bay Club and Marina in an exclusive residential area of Miami. Four ladies talked Neil into impersonating Dolly Parton at the party. "They dressed him in a blonde wig, a red dress, and a pair of Charles Jourdan shoes with four-inch chrome heels." Neil won the prize for the best costume that night. As a result, his picture was posted on the club's bulletin board.[19]

Some months later, George and Em Crook of Nashville happened to be at the club where they saw the photograph on the bulletin board. Em said, "My God, that's Neil Cargile." So, the word of Neil being dressed as Dolly Parton got back to Nashville. Slowly, rumors of other cross-dressing excursions by Neil began to circulate in town. "The other occasions were costume parties, too; they were always out of town," stated a profile of Neil in *The New Yorker*. "But then Cargile began to dress up in Nashville. At first, he did it at private parties and with a degree of subtlety. He'd wear a blazer, a shirt and tie—and a kilt. Instead of the traditional knee-length woolen socks, however, he'd put on black stockings and high heels; or he'd wear the kilt and the heels with a formal dinner jacket." Neil finally had what he called a Vice-Versa party at his home; guests were asked to come dressed as a member of the opposite sex. Cargile came in drag. His girlfriend came dressed as Sir Lancelot; she rode into the house on a pony. The party and other sightings of Neil Cargile in drag caused a great deal of talk around town, but it was not until the 1979 Cumberland Caper costume party, *The New Yorker* recalled, "that Nashville got a good look at Neil Cargile as a cross-dresser." The theme for the party that year was for everybody to come dressed as their favorite character. While couples came in a variety of disguises, such as George and Martha Washington or Marie Antoinette and Louis XVI, Neil wore a blue dress and a long, blonde wig. When asked who he came as, he said, "As Neil Cargile in a dress." Some of Neil's close friends asked him if he had lost his mind. Neil assured them that he was not gay but was simply having a good time. Once, when another man came to a Cumberland Caper dressed as Dustin Hoffman in *Tootsie*, Cargile was incensed and swore not to return to the benefit event if someone was going to horn in on his act.[20]

Neil liked to shop for ladies' clothing at the Bargain Boutique, a popular secondhand ladies clothing store in Green Hills. He loved to come out of the dressing room in a ladies' skirt and surprise whoever was shopping there. Then, he would diffuse the situation by asking the customers what they thought of his skirt. Of course, word quickly got back to Neil's family that he was a cross-dresser. Neil also occasionally bought ladies' attire at Stein Mart on Nolensville Road. Woozie Blair, who worked there on Saturdays and some evenings in the late 1970s and early 1980s, remembers that the store managers allowed Neil to use the ladies' dressing room when trying on something rather than have him carry the clothes across the store to the men's dressing room. By this time,

Mr. Cargile Sr. had died. Had he been alive, Neil said, "He'd have killed me." When Mrs. Cargile heard about what her son was doing, she confronted him, saying, "You are the best looking man in Nashville, Neil. Why on earth would you want to dress up in women's clothes?" Neil replied, "It's fun, Mom." When asked about his brother Allen's reaction, Neil said, "He's a born-again Christian, so of course, he hates it."[21]

On the second Saturday in May 1977, Jesse "Easy" Henley's horse Alvaro the Second won the Iroquois Steeplechase with Dwight Hall riding. At the post-Steeplechase victory party at Green Acres, Margaret Currey and "Easy" Henley's lovely farm in Brentwood, Neil crashed the party by landing his helicopter and stepping out in a sports coat, tie, skirt and high heels.

On another occasion, Brownlee Currey Jr. was outside the front of his home on Sneed Road in Williamson County when he heard a loud motor and the whirling of wings. He was astonished to see Neil Cargile land his helicopter in Brownlee's driveway. Neil stepped out and asked Brownlee if he wanted to go for a ride. Brownlee declined.

Once, when Julia Reed, who lived in New Orleans, came for a Christmas visit, she was at the Belle Meade Country Club with her grandfather, Dan Brooks. As they were walking down the corridor, they passed Neil, who was dressed in women's clothing. He and Dan spoke, and Mr. Brooks acted as if this was not unusual. Julia was, however, astounded and asked her grandfather, "What in the world is going on?" He explained that Neil was a member of the club and often dressed that way, even though he was not a homosexual.

Jeweler Michael Corzine has colorful Neil Cargile stories, too. Mike recalled once that, "while I was in Italy for a couple of months, Joe Erwin and David White had redecorated my house. About a day after I got back, I decided it looked so good I would have a cocktail party. Neil came, uninvited, in a big red dress and a big old wig and a hat. I didn't notice it during the night, but I later learned he was dancing on top of this marble coffee table with his girlfriend, whose name, I think, was Peaches. The next morning when I got up, my maid said, 'Your coffee table is cracked all the way down the middle.' I called Joe and David and they assured me it had not been cracked when they put it in. I called my good friend Wally Graham, and he said, 'Neil broke it, dancing on it last night.' So, I called Neil, and I said, 'You have just broken a $3,500 coffee table, and I want you to pay for it.' When he said he didn't have any idea of paying for it, I called my attorneys at Bass, Berry and Sims. They wouldn't handle my claim because he was also a client of theirs. Finally, I called Neil again. I said, 'Everybody knows that you broke the coffee table dancing around on it last night. I've just got to tell you that in that big blond wig and that big Gucci dress and that Hermes belt and those Jourdan shoes, you are a very big woman.' And he said, 'I am, aren't I?' And he sent me a check. But I think it was only because I flattered him."[22]

Speaking of shoes, it has always been a treat for Lynn (Mrs. Jack) May to shop in Atlanta. One day, while trying on shoes in an upscale ladies' store, Lynn looked up and saw Neil sitting across from her trying on a pair of size eleven red pumps with very high heels. Despite her surprise, Lynn kept her composure and complimented Neil on his choice.[23]

———

Once, when Neil's mother was in the back seat of her son's jet, his landing gear would not come down as he began his approach to the Nashville International Airport. He did not tell her about the problem and landed the plane on a grass strip. When safely down, Mrs. Cargile said, "Neil, that is the roughest landing you ever made."[24] Likely not.

———

Neil is also said to have pulled friends on water skis behind his Piper Cub float plane along the Cumberland River. He kept it at Rock Harbor Marina; it had a sixty-five horsepower engine.

———

In 1979, Neil flew his plane from Nashville to New Orleans with two passengers. Almost as soon as the plane came to a stop in New Orleans, one of them, Terry Walls, an insurance executive, jumped out to see about their rental car. Cargile later said, "We told him to go back around the propellers, but evidently he had been drinking before he got on the plane and we didn't know it." He walked out of the plane and directly into the still-whirling left propeller, decapitating himself. Mr. Cargile felt he did everything he could to prevent the tragic accident. Although no charges were filed, Walls' widow filed a civil suit against Neil in Nashville Circuit Court in 1980. Cargile said the suit was settled out of court four years later. He did not reveal the settlement.[25]

On a flight from New Orleans to Nashville a decade later, Neil's single-engine Mooney began to vibrate violently about forty miles from the Nashville airport. He suspected that one of his propeller blades had broken off, as it had been repaired a few months earlier. He radioed the air controller in Nashville that he was in difficulty, losing altitude, and that his instrument panel was vibrating so violently that he could not read it. Nashville cleared him to land at the Murfreesboro airport, only three miles away. Neil could not do that, as his plane was already clipping the tops of trees. Suddenly, Interstate 24 loomed in front of him. Realizing this was his best chance, Neil landed on the interstate embankment. He did so skillfully, but the speed of the plane caused it to veer on to the highway, skidding into east-bound traffic on its belly with its landing gear still up. He saw three headlights coming directly at him. Two of the cars swerved to the side and avoided being hit. As he tried to steer his plane to the median strip, a wing caught underneath the third car, a van, and dragged it to the median with his plane. No one was hurt, the van had only minor damages, but the Mooney was wrecked. Emergency vehicles reached the scene promptly and began spraying foam on the huge puddle of gasoline that spilled on the interstate. Television crews also arrived and filmed the scene for the ten o'clock evening news. When a reporter asked the calm and collected Neil, "What caused the crash?" Neil smiled and said, "I like being the center of attention." Aviation officials, also on the scene, praised him for his skill in landing the plane. His cool demeanor, more than forty years of flying experience, and his incredible survival skills prevented a much more serious accident.[26]

Neil Cargile Jr. standing beside his wrecked plane, March 1990. Photo courtesy of the Nashville Public Library, Special Collections.

At the time of his interstate landing, Neil was sixty-one years old. One article on the crash described him as "impressively handsome, with glinting blue eyes, a square jaw, and white hair that fell casually across his forehead."

⚬⚬⚬

In 1993, the *Palm Beach Daily News* published an article titled "Palm Beach Style: There are No Rules." Neil was the first of five stylish men profiled. The article said, "No, it's not Dame Edna. It's SheNeil (pronounced chenille) and he dresses to thrill. One of his typical outfits is a blazer and a miniskirt. This Au Bar regular is in a class all his own and loves to dance the night away."[27]

The word quickly got back to Nashville when Neil won a trophy in the Easter Bonnet contest at the Palm Beach Polo and Country Club. "The matrons at the club were furious that their daughters and granddaughters had been exposed to a grown man in a blazer, a miniskirt and high heels—not to mention a broad-brimmed, lace-festooned, flowered straw hat." The affair had been written up in the *Palm Beach Daily News;* Neil's Nashville friends were not that surprised. Em Crook's reaction was simply: "That's Neil." Neil had explained that he cross-dressed because it was fun, but Jimmy Armistead's response was this: "Saying it's fun is OK for the first few parties, but after twenty years there has to be a better reason." Frank Jarman, who had enormous respect for Neil, felt that cross-dressing was just another one of Neil's adventures. "I think he just got bored."[28]

In the spring of 1994, writer John Berendt visited Nashville. While in town, he heard about Neil Cargile Jr. Intrigued with what he heard, Berendt discovered that Neil, having gone through a second marriage, "was living with his girlfriend in Palm Beach, where some of his dredging operations were located." The following August, Berendt called Neil and asked to meet him to learn more about his motivation for dressing in drag. Cargile was open to the idea and they agreed to meet in New York City a couple of weeks later when Cargile would be up there with his girlfriend, Dorothy Koss. Neil would be in New York to seek financing for a gold-dredging operation he hoped to launch in South America. Berendt and Neil met at Neil's room at the Algonquin Hotel. When Neil opened the door to his room, Berendt saw a "towering, broad-shouldered figure" standing before him. Cargile was wearing a tight blue-sequined dress, rhinestone-encrusted sunglasses, blue earrings, a wide-brimmed straw hat, high heels and panty hose. He had makeup splotched on his face and bright-red lipstick casually smeared across his lips. Dorothy came out of the bathroom to meet Berendt. She was a pretty blonde with "wavy hair, smooth skin, and makeup that was applied as artfully as Cargile's was not." She seemed to be in her forties. Neil called her "baaad." "She encourages me to be wilder and wilder," he said. Dorothy responded, "Well, you know how I feel about it, SheNeil. If you're going to take the trouble to dress up, why look like a frumpy old matron?" Just as the three of them were about to leave for dinner, the telephone rang. Berendt listened and heard Neil say, "That river is full of gold and right now the Venezuelans have got men out there panning for it with shovels. The computer-controlled dredge I designed can do in

From left to right, Dorothy Koss, Neil Cargile Jr., and Holly Armistead at the Everglades Club. Photo courtesy of Holly (Mrs. William J., Jr.) Anderson.

one hour what it takes a thousand men all day to do by hand. No kidding, and the beauty of it is we get to keep the gold. We give the Venezuelans ten percent of what we sell it for, and then we take a fourteen percent mining depletion write-off on our U.S. taxes. We're getting offers to do the same thing worldwide, you know." Neil said all the details were in some papers he sent the man and then asked about the caller's wife, who had the flu. Neil's advice was "Tell her to take four times the dose of whatever the doctor prescribes. Knock the hell out of it. That's what I do. What the hell do doctors know anyway? They are much too cautious."[29]

After Neil got off the phone, it wasn't long before the inevitable question about Neil's motivation for dressing in drag came up again. In the car on the way to the restaurant, Dorothy said she had gradually come around to accept Neil's cross-dressing. "I wish he didn't cross-dress, but I won't try to change him. To me, he's a combination of Crocodile Dundee, Rambo, and Jezebel." At the restaurant, the Tribeca Grill, their waitress winked at Neil and said,

"I'd kill for legs like yours." Over dinner, Cargile spoke unre-
servedly about cross-dressing. He said, "Men are forced to wear a
uniform that never changes: a jacket and trousers. Women can wear
anything they want, and it's OK. I happen to be more comfortable
in a dress than in a blazer and slacks. And anyway, I'm a big show-
off. I have a motto: 'If you aren't doing something different, you
aren't doing anything at all.' That's the way I've always lived. When
my cross-dressing got to be too much for my wife, she made me go
to a psychiatrist. So I went to see Dr. Joseph Fishbein, an associate
professor of psychiatry at Vanderbilt University. The first thing
Fishbein asked me was, did I like men? I said no. Then, he told me
some of his colleagues were cross-dressers, too. They'd come home
at night and put on their wives' clothes. And they were doctors! I
got the impression that Fishbein didn't think there was very much
wrong with me. Anyhow, I never went back."

That same evening, Neil expanded on his thoughts about the
propriety of cross-dressing. He told Berendt that there were some
places he would never wear a dress. "I wouldn't go to church in a
dress, and I wouldn't go to the Belle Meade Country Club or the
Palm Beach Bath and Tennis Club in drag, either.[30] Those places are
hallowed ground. But I'm not afraid of going anywhere in drag, if
that's what you mean. I know it blows people away, but that's part
of what makes it fun. Of course, once in a while I've had to set
people straight. Like, one night a couple of years ago I walked into
a bar and heard a guy mutter, 'Faggot.' Well, I just turned to him and
said as nicely as I could, 'I'm Neil Cargile, and I don't think we've
met.' I put out my hand, and he shook it. Now, I'm a mechanical
engineer, and I work with my hands a lot. So, I squeezed that man's
hand. Hard. I crunched. I cracked. And I kept on squeezing until his
eyes bugged out and his body writhed and he let out the most pitiful
gasp of pain. I haven't had any trouble with him since."[31]

Berendt suggested that they meet next at Tavern on the Green in
Central Park. Neil was enthusiastic. "Sounds perfect. Dorothy will
love it." Berendt suggested that Neil go not in drag. Although Neil
agreed, when Berendt saw Neil and Dorothy get out of the cab at
Tavern on the Green, Cargile was wearing a blazer and open-necked
shirt, as well as "a black-and-white striped micro mini skirt, panty
hose, and heels." Neil jauntily said, "I thought I'd come half and

half." After they were seated, other guests noticed Neil's attire. Two women from Sao Paulo, Brazil, came by and asked Neil to pose for them. Other diners were encouraged by this scene and got up to watch, as did several waiters. Neil was radiant with the attention he received. He said, "Did you see how everyone enjoyed themselves? That always happens when we go out in Palm Beach. The party doesn't start until I arrive. I am the entertainment. Dorothy and I have been talking about opening a club in Palm Beach. We'd call it Club SheNeil."[32]

The next day, Berendt, Dorothy—whom Neil called "Sweet Pea"—and SheNeil went to New York's premier shopping mart for cross-dressers and drag queens. There, Neil started trying on dresses with Dorothy taking pictures. The salesman got annoyed because the store had a lot of guys come in, try on dresses, have their pictures taken and then leave without buying anything. He asked "Are you going to buy something?" Neil said, "Well, we're not sure yet." The salesman had already told Dorothy that picture taking was forbidden. Finally, he had enough and asked them to leave. On the way out, Neil said, "The hell with him. He thinks trying on dresses is fun. It isn't. It's hard physical labor. You can work up a sweat doing it." Dorothy laughed and joked, "Of all the places to be thrown out of a store, we had to pick one that caters to cross-dressers."[33]

Later in 1994, Berendt met Dorothy and Neil in Palm Beach, where the three went for drinks at the home of one of Neil's investors in his gold-dredging venture in Venezuela. "Neil wore a seersucker suit, a subdued tie and white wing-tip shoes." Unknown to their host, Neil also had on panty hose under his suit and a corset under his shirt. After a forty-five minute visit, they rose to leave. The host paused at the door and asked Neil how old he was. He then answered his own question. "Sixty-five? Sixty-six? Tell me, Neil, why on earth would a man your age and in your position want to leave a beautiful place like Palm Beach and go into the goddamn jungle and muck around for gold?" Neil put his hand on the man's shoulder and said, "It's real simple. No Environmental Protection Agency, no IRS, no unions, no attorneys. Besides—and don't tell me you don't know this already—the world's currencies are headed for the dumper, and when they get there gold will be king again." The man smiled, shook his head and saw them out. That evening, after dinner, Neil put on a red dress and his long blond wig and went out on the town with Dorothy. At each bar they visited, Neil and Dorothy would step on an empty dance floor, and, within minutes, many of the other patrons would be on the floor, having a good time. Neil said it always worked that way.[34]

Berendt's article on Neil appeared in *The New Yorker* Magazine in January 1995. Berendt was insightful. It came "complete with photos of Cargile in a business suit and in the festive female outfit of 'SheNeil,' as he called his female alter-ego." Nashvillians made a run on local bookstores to get a copy. A few months later, organizers of Nashville's annual Oyster Easter Benefit nominated Cargile both Oyster King and Oyster Queen.

John Bransford Jr., a lifelong friend of Neil's, was asked how he felt about Neil's cross-dressing. John said, "When I first heard of it, I nearly fell out of my chair. I asked him what the hell he did it for, and he said he enjoyed the excitement of it." John continued, "In every other way, he was normal as can be. I can tell you this: Neil was totally and completely heterosexual."[35]

One evening, about a year and a half before Neil died, he and John Seigenthaler were having dinner at the Sunset Grill in Nashville when an employee brought a phone to the table with a call for Neil. John could hear only Neil's half of the conversation. "I'm tired. I don't want to." "No, no." "OK, I'll come in about an hour." John asked, "What was that all about?" Neil said someone was having a party and they wanted him to come "cross-dressed."[36]

⋙⋘

Not long before his death, Neil returned to Nashville from Guyana, where he said he had "dumped every penny" he had into a failed business venture. While there, he contracted a fatal case of malaria. A week before his death he was supposed to go on trial in Palm Beach on a drunk-driving charge. He had been arrested there in the summer of 1994. When pulled over by the police, Cargile was wearing a red dress and was accompanied by his girlfriend Dorothy. They had been at a dance club earlier in the evening. Cargile, who was represented by the public defender, told the *Palm Beach Post* that he didn't show up for the trial because of the malaria and a fever of one hundred and two degrees. Cargile's brother Allen said he had been misdiagnosed with a different kind of malaria, and his situation took a turn for the worse. He died on August 2, 1995, survived by his daughter and son.[37]

Up until the time of his death in a Palm Beach hospital, Neil remained president of American Marine and Machinery Company, a Nashville manufacturer of dredging equipment.[38]

Neil's Nashville friends were stunned at his passing. They knew there was a possibility that he would die prematurely, but thought, if that happened, it would be the result of an airplane crash or some other horrific accident because of the aggressive, flamboyant way Neil lived his life. No one thought he would succumb to malaria. John Bransford Jr. admitted, "I didn't think anything could kill him, as tough as he was. I would not have been surprised if he had died in an air crash, but I was really surprised that a disease got him. He was a hell of a nice guy, and very bright. He was about as good an engineer as I've ever seen in my life—extremely creative. He lived life fully; I'll tell you that. He never forgot his old friends, even though he'd taken up a different life."[39]

Chapter 4

Dudley Clark Fort Sr.
1911–1994

Easter would never have been the same without Sunday dinner at the Belle Meade Country Club after church. The club was always crowded with people—men in their best, ladies with their bonnets, little girls in dresses with lace and ruffles, and little boys in suits. Uncle Dudley Fort and his wife Pearl would always be there. He wasn't actually my uncle, but that's what all of us in my generation called him. I remember him weaving his way through the crowd, smiling and speaking to everyone in his distinctive voice. At Easter, he often wore a loud sports coat that looked liked Joseph's legendary coat of many colors. Everyone was aware of his genial presence. I can still visualize him kissing the ladies, shaking hands, and joking with his golf buddies and the other men, nearly all of whom he knew.

Dudley Clark Fort was born December 2, 1911, the second of five children of Dr. and Mrs. Rufus Elijah Fort, whose 350-acre farm, Fortland, was one of the showplaces of Davidson County. The farm lay on the west side of the Cumberland River, four miles northeast of town. There, Dr. Fort developed a herd of Jersey cattle considered one of the best in the country. He had a brilliant career as a physician and surgeon in private practice in Nashville before joining National Life and Accident Insurance Company on a full-time basis about 1920. One of the five founders of the company in 1901, he was a member of the original board of directors of National Life. For many years, Dr. Fort was vice president and medical director of the company. On his death in 1940, my father, Jesse Wills, who was then vice-president of National Life, wrote of him: "Dr. Fort was the most steadfast of friends, and in the same way he was a firm foe of all that he considered wrong." Dr. Fort's wife was the former Louise Clark of Boston, whose mother had grown up in Cross Plains, Tennessee. In addition to Dudley, the children included Rufus E. Fort Jr., Dr. Garth E. Fort, Cornelia Fort, and Louise Fort.

One Saturday in the summer of 1925, when Dudley Fort was fourteen and his brother Garth was twelve or so, Dudley was planning to go to town and see some of his friends. Those plans were nipped in the bud at eight o'clock that morning, when Dr. Fort told Dudley and Garth to go out in the front yard and remove the crabgrass instead. That was a problem, as the front yard was two acres. Dr. Fort was frustrated because, until his wife planted roses in the front yard, it was covered by a perfect stand of Kentucky fescue. He had tried unsuccessfully to remove the crabgrass by several schemes, including having a man come in with a steam engine equipped with pods he placed over the grass. The idea was to kill the crabgrass with steam, but it didn't work. The alternative was for Dudley and Garth to dig up the obnoxious stuff.

It was hot that morning, and when Dudley and Garth returned to the front porch at noon to tell their father that they had cleared the lawn of the crabgrass, they were near exhaustion. Dr. Fort initially accepted their report, but then gazed across his beautiful lawn and said, "I believe I see a little crabgrass in the north corner." He then told his boys to remove it. Dudley had suffered enough. He blurted out, "I'm through. I'm not doing this to my health." Garth could not believe his ears. Dr. Fort heard loud and clear. He grabbed Dudley by the arm and dragged him to the upstairs of the barn where he found a buggy whip. He then whipped Dudley with the plank end. The next day, one of the field hands asked Dudley if they had seen a snake in the barn, because he had heard such blood-curdling sounds coming from the barn the day before. Dudley was so outraged by being whipped that he later returned to the barn and chopped the whip into six-inch segments.

On another occasion, a teenaged Dudley invited his friend Ollie Minton out to Fortland. Intent on having fun, they managed to capture a pigeon. Thinking it would be amusing, they taped a sparkler to the pigeon's leg, lit it, and then released the bird. It promptly flew into the barn, where sparks caught the hay on fire and burned the barn down.[1] Although he did not intend to burn the barn, Dudley had his revenge.

After graduating from Wallace University School in Nashville, Dudley entered Virginia Military Institute in 1930. That year, his older brother, Rufus Fort Jr., had already graduated from VMI and was teaching math and managing the riding academy there. One day in his plebe year, Dudley, whose nickname was "Speedy," was walking off demerits in the rain. He did not like this and thought, "My father would not approve of them doing this to me." Dudley left VMI following his freshman year after failing English and French. He took both courses that summer at Peabody College and Vanderbilt University, respectively. Having passed both, he registered at the University of the South on September 15, 1931, as a sophomore.[2] Dudley was influenced to do so because his father graduated from Sewanee Military Academy and attended the University of the South from 1887 until 1889 before receiving a medical degree from Vanderbilt in 1894.[3] Outgoing and gregarious, Dudley pledged Phi Delta Theta and played on their intramural baseball team the following spring. That same year, Dudley's younger brother Garth matriculated at VMI, where he would graduate in 1935. Dudley returned to Sewanee in September 1932, but withdrew from school following the Christmas break. While at the University of the South, his best grades were in public speaking.[4] On a personal history completed by Sewanee alumni in 1941, there was a space for "other activities." Dudley wrote there, "Well, I did enjoy the dances."

Again, following in the footsteps of his father and his older brother Rufus, who had recently left VMI to join National Life and Accident Insurance Company as an agent, Dudley joined the company as an agent in Akron, Ohio, on January 30, 1933, when he was twenty-two years old. Dudley's father gave him a used car when he left for Akron. As he drove away from Fortland, Dudley realized that his father was crying, something he had never seen before.

Selling life and accident insurance on a debit in Akron in the middle of the Great Depression wasn't easy. One of the ways Dudley learned to identify men prosperous enough to afford a policy was to see if they smoked. If someone had a cigar in his mouth, Dudley figured he could afford a small policy.[5]

After working in Akron for eleven months, Dudley was transferred to an Atlanta district office at year's end.[6] There, in 1934, he kept telling his superintendent, "This is how we did it in Akron." The superintendent got tired of hearing this and said, "Dudley, it would have been better if you hadn't gone to Akron." But Dudley was a good life insurance salesman, and was promoted to superintendent on January 21, 1935.[7] His next promotion was to manager of the Atlanta Number Three District in 1940.[8]

In the meantime, despite not having graduated from either VMI or the University of the South, Dudley was active in the Atlanta VMI alumni chapter, and would become president of the Sewanee Club of Atlanta.

Sometime after moving to Atlanta, Dudley hurt his hand and needed the attention of a physician. Remembering that his father had told him, when he first moved to Atlanta, to look up Dr. Fort's old friend and distant cousin, Dr. Arthur G. Fort, Dudley made an appointment to see the internist. While in Dr. Fort's office, Dudley saw a photograph of a pretty young woman. He asked Dr. Fort who she was. Dr. Fort said she was his daughter and that her name was Victoria Pearl Fort. Dudley met, courted and fell in love with Pearl. They married in Atlanta on April 9, 1935, at St. Luke's Episcopal Church, her family's church, which Dudley also attended. Pearl was a graduate of the Chicago Academy of Fine Arts and had studied at the Sorbonne in Paris and the Parsons School of Design in New York. Dudley and Pearl lived at 1729 North Decatur Road for twenty-five years. They had two sons, Dudley C. Fort Jr., born April 10, 1936, and Arthur G. Fort II, born July 29, 1937.

During the nearly twenty-seven years the Forts lived in Atlanta, Dudley worked for National Life, enjoyed fox hunting with the Atlanta Hunt Club, and played golf several times a week at the Piedmont Driving Club where he was a member. In 1941, he wrote that his avocation was keeping honeybee hives. He also served, in 1948, as president of the Atlanta Life Underwriters Association and

Uncle Dudley Fort standing with julep cups on a silver tray in Atlanta, Georgia. Photo courtesy of Arthur G. Fort II.

in 1958, as president of the Georgia Society of the Sons of the American Revolution. At that time, his office was in a company-owned building at 630 Lee Street SW.

On February 22, 1950, Dudley hit the pinnacle of social success in Atlanta when he was crowned King of the Mardi Gras Ball at the Piedmont Driving Club.[9] Pearl kept up by having her own radio show and serving as president of the Atlanta Chapter of American Women in Radio and Television.

Meanwhile in Nashville, Dudley's brothers Rufus Jr. and Garth were on their way to establishing distinguished careers at National Life. Rufus later became a senior vice president in charge of selling and servicing life insurance, while Garth became senior vice president and medical director, following in the footsteps of his father.

Dudley's sister Cornelia attended Ward-Belmont and Sarah Lawrence College, where she received a diploma as a two-year graduate on June 10, 1939. Cornelia then returned to Nashville, where she became a member of the Girls' Cotillion Club, the Junior League and the Query Club, a literary group. She also rode horses with Dudley, who introduced her to fox hunting, a sport she came to enjoy. Soon after graduation, Cornelia bested her brothers by learning to fly. Her father had told his sons never to fly, but he didn't think to warn his daughters about the dangers of doing so. Falling in love with flying, Cornelia, in rapid succession, received her private and commercial pilot's licenses and instructor's rating. She was instructing a student over Pearl Harbor when an attacking Japanese plane missed hitting her plane by a few feet. Cornelia became the second woman to volunteer for the Women's Auxiliary Ferrying Squadron, a forerunner of the WASPs that had responsibility for ferrying fighters and bombers to points of embarkation. On a routine ferrying flight in March 1943, Cornelia died at the controls of a 450-horsepower Vultee aircraft when an Army aviator's plane struck hers and caused it to crash. She was the first of thirty-eight women in military service to die in World War II.[10] Cornelia's death devastated her parents. When Cornelia Fort Airport was dedicated to his deceased sister in 1945, Dudley was one of the speakers. For the occasion, military helicopters flew over the ceremonies in formation before landing. A marker at Cornelia Fort Airport honoring Cornelia bears her quote: "I am grateful that my one talent, flying, was useful to my country."

Louise, the youngest of the five Fort children, idolized her older sister. Just as Cornelia had done, Louise also went to Sarah Lawrence College. Later, Louise married Donald Linton, whose family owned the Linton Pencil Company in Shelbyville, Tennessee. She never got into flying.

One day, Dudley came from Atlanta to the home office accompanied by his personal attorney. My father, then executive vice president of National Life, was puzzled why Dudley needed an attorney. He asked Dudley, but never got an answer that made sense.

One day in 1957, Dudley and a wealthy Atlanta landowner went fox hunting. Suddenly, Dudley's friend had a fatal heart attack and fell from his horse dead. That death made a strong impression on Dudley, who decided that there was more to life than work, work, work. He then went to England on a lengthy vacation. About this time, Pearl was also frustrated. Her concern was with Dudley going out at night without her. Thinking a move back to Nashville would help the situation, she asked her brothers-in-law, Rufus and Garth, to use their influence to have Dudley transferred to the home office. Instead, Dudley took early retirement from National Life and moved back to Nashville in 1960, where he bought a handsome house on Herbert Place. Dudley was able to buy the house because, as he said, "Over the years I acquired a respectable amount of National Life stock, which appreciated considerably." Dudley then joked, "In fact, I remember someone telling me once, 'You can be a millionaire in National Life stock and still not have enough dividends to buy groceries.'"[11]

Dudley and Pearl lived for the balance of their lives at Horseshoe Hill, 4411 Herbert Place in Belle Meade. During the 1960s, he was working in real estate. By the time she moved to Nashville, Pearl was a gifted flower designer who enjoyed demonstrating her art at flower shows and traveling across the country as a flower show judge. She also became a member of the Garden Club of Nashville and the Garden Club of America (GCA). She was once honored by the GCA with a medal of recognition for her flower arranging skills. In 1967, Pearl wrote a book, *A Complete Guide to Flower Arranging,* published by Viking Press. More and more, she did her thing and Dudley did his.

When Dudley's son Arthur returned home from military duty in 1960, Mr. Fort said to him, "Arthur, this family can afford one 'sport.' That's me. You've got to go to work." Arthur got a job with National Life, starting on a debit in Chattanooga just as his father had done in Akron in 1933.[12]

———◦◦◦———

Margaret Sloan, a longtime friend of Dudley and Pearl, saw a great deal of Dudley at Hillsboro Hounds events. She described him as a "feeler." She meant he had a tendency to put his hands on women who were attractive. For this reason, she had given him a wide berth when he was in school. In Dudley's defense, he had an outgoing personality, admittedly enjoyed women, and was known to use his hands to express himself. Unquestionably, Dudley and Pearl both liked to be the center of attention and were somewhat competitive. At those Easter Sunday dinners at the Belle Meade Country Club, Dudley and his brother Rufus usually had on the loudest sports coats and slacks in the club. Dudley loved joking with his friends there. And they, in turn, enjoyed his company. People simply liked Dudley.

———◦◦◦———

Dudley was definitely a ham. At a 1963 awards dinner given by Theatre Nashville, he won the "best supporting actor award," for the dapper courtliness he displayed as Beauregard Jackson Pickett Burnside, a fox-hunting Southern gentleman from Peckerwood Plantation, Georgia, in a production of *Auntie Mame.*[13]

The truth is that if something interesting was going on, Dudley instinctively wanted to get involved. Once, when Harold Vanderbilt was chairman of the Vanderbilt Board of Trust, he invited a number of Nashville trustees and their wives to fly at his expense to the Kentucky Derby. The Louisville Vanderbilt Club had a dinner for the Vanderbilt alumni who either lived there or were in town for the occasion. Margaret Sloan, wife of VU Board Member John Sloan, was seated next to Mr. Vanderbilt at the head table. Dudley Fort, not a Vanderbilt alumnus, happened to be at the country club that evening. He saw his Nashville friends and asked one of them, "What are you doing here?" Whomever he approached told Dudley about the VU Club dinner. A little later, during cocktails, Dudley slipped into the room where the Vanderbilt group would dine and put his name on a card at the head table. He then sat there for the dinner. Fred Russell realized that Uncle Dudley had crashed the party. So, after dinner, he told Dudley that they were charging the dinner to him.[14]

If Vanderbilt didn't welcome Uncle Dudley at its alumni affairs, the University of the South certainly did. Along with his wife who was an accomplished hostess, Uncle Dudley hosted, throughout the 1960s and 1970s, annual Christmas season cocktail parties at his home for the Sewanee Club of Nashville and prospective students. In 1965, he was president of the Sewanee Club of Nashville when the club won the Dobbins Trophy in recognition of being the best Sewanee Club in the country.[15]

In December of 1965, Dudley told Sewanee officials that he and Pearl had decided to give a stained glass window to All Saints' Chapel in memory of his parents. Pearl supervised the design and the installation of "the healing window" that was on the north wall of the chapel.[16] In 1973, Dudley worked with Arthur Ben Chitty and Rick Holton, his own trust officer at Third National Bank, to set up a charitable remainder unitrust with the university as beneficiary.

———⊷∘⊶———

Uncle Dudley was an enthusiastic member of the Hillsboro Hounds and rode at their hunts for many years. He always wore a top hat and rode a magnificent horse named Ironsides that must have been seventeen hands high. Dudley also was well known on the horse show circuit. In August 1962, Dudley's horse won two blue ribbons with him riding at the Tennessee State Horse Show at the Ellington Agricultural Center in Nashville. On Labor Day 1963, he rode his Irish hunter, Waterford, at the Chattanooga Charity Horse Show.[17] In 1961, Uncle Dudley served as chief patrol judge of the Iroquois Memorial Steeplechase. For years, he led a group of young people horseback riding on the morning of the Fourth of July. *The Nashville Tennessean* featured a picture of Dudley leading Cayce McAlister; Mrs. Charles Curran of Sewanee; Rodes Hart Jr.; Daniel Curran; and Harry Hill McAlister on such a ride in 1966. That year, the group ended the ride at the home of Dudley's sister, Louise Linton, on Chickering Road.[18]

Dudley's riding days ended abruptly when he fell off his horse and broke some ribs. His physician told him that, if he fell off again, he might be paralyzed. Dudley gave up riding cold turkey, got rid of his riding habit, and put his horses to pasture at his sister Louise's house.[19]

Once, Dudley was a guest at an elegant wedding rehearsal dinner at an expensive home on Lookout Mountain. Because there were a lot of out-of-town attendees, the master of ceremonies asked everyone to introduce him or herself. After several men introduced themselves as being from Lookout Mountain, Tennessee, or Lookout Mountain, Georgia, Uncle Dudley, in his turn, said he was from Belle Meade, Tennessee.

Politically, Dudley was conservative. Only two generations away from the Civil War, he was a devotee of the ideology referred to as the "Lost Cause." This embraced the idea that the Southern states had a constitutional right to secede from the national union and that the Civil War was the result of Northern aggression. Not surprisingly, Dudley was named, in 1965, as a Brigadier of the Confederate Air Cavalry. To qualify, applicants had to be sympathetic to the Confederate cause and own a fighting horse. Dudley qualified on both counts.[20] Arthur Ben Chitty of Sewanee presented the commission. In 1967, when the question of returning the Panama Canal to the Panamanians was a hot topic, Dudley was against giving it away.

—————<small>⌖</small>—————

Dudley was a regular on the Belle Meade Country Club golf course for many years. He often played there with Father Albert Siener, Jimmy Hofstead and Bill Bainbridge. Dudley said his handicap was twenty-one, but "I can never shoot it." Dudley and his golfing friends were, however, wonderful storytellers; it was always a treat to be invited to play in their foursome as a guest. Dudley had a driver made to his specifications; some of his friends thought it might be illegal. He often carried some bread with him to feed the ducks. They came to expect him when he crossed the creek on the fifteenth hole.

In addition to playing Belle Meade, Dudley also enjoyed playing golf at other clubs, such as Turtle Point on Lake Wilson in North Alabama. Father Siener, Bill Bainbridge, Ollie Minton and other golfing buddies would usually accompany Dudley on his golf trips. One time, a friend asked him if he was going to take Pearl. He joked, "Hell, no. This is a pleasure trip."

Dudley did not always leave Pearl at home. In 1981 he took her with him to the Southern Seniors Golf Association Tournament in Naples, Florida. Although he did not win the tournament, he did win a jacket. Once, a friend mentioned to Dudley that he would rather be lucky than rich. Dudley quipped, "I'm both."

One Easter morning when Uncle Dudley and Father Siener were playing at Belle Meade, another golfer said "Happy Easter." Father Siener said, "Happy Easter to you, but don't tell anybody you saw us." Uncle Dudley, who was extremely fond of Father Siener, claimed Siener had a drive-through confessional at the Cathedral of the Incarnation and that it had a sign that said: "Toot and tell or go to Hell."[21] Dudley's fondness for Father Siener prompted him to give a good deal of money to the Catholic church.

Willie Gibbons, the longtime golf professional at the Belle Meade Country Club, was a good friend of Uncle Dudley's as well. Occasionally, they would take out-of-town trips together. On a trip to Kentucky to watch Fort's huge horse Big Divot race, Willie was talking to the African-American hostler in the stable while Dudley

Uncle Dudley Fort feeding a duck from his golf cart at the Belle Meade Country Club, October 28, 1982. Photo courtesy of the Nashville Public Library, Special Collections.

was holding court elsewhere. When Willie asked the man how long he had worked for Dudley, he said, "A long time." Willie followed up by asking if Dudley worked. The hostler replied, "Naw. Uncle Dudley and work parted company a long time ago."[22]

During the 1970s, Dudley and the other members of his foursome would often have breakfast at Bill Bainbridge's house. Bill's son Tom would sit in and enjoy the conversations that were usually humorous and often salty. Once, Uncle Dudley showed Tom a photograph of some young woman he knew. Tom remembered that her nickname was "Lamb Chop."[23]

Occasionally, Tom and his dad would have breakfast at Uncle Dudley's. Tom recalled in 2009 that invariably Uncle Dudley would serve them half of a dove's breast and an egg.

———✦———

In May 1982, Pearl suffered a stroke. The following March, Dudley wrote a friend at Sewanee, "Pearl is getting somewhat stronger and does not need as much assistance as she has in the past ten months. However, she has two nurses every day and a therapist comes three or four times a week." Still confined to a wheelchair in the spring of 1988, Pearl's condition deteriorated precipitously. On January 7, 1990, Uncle Dudley wrote his good friend Arthur Ben Chitty to say, "My sweet Pearl is at death's door in the Franklin County Health Care Center and I try to see her once or twice a week and it is a wrench on my heart strings."[24] Pearl Fort died February 16, 1990.

A longtime member of the Nashville Chapter of the English-Speaking Union, Dudley served as president from 1982 until 1984. He was also an active member of St. George's Episcopal Church.

In May 1993, Dudley wrote C. Beeler Brush in the office of Planned Giving at the University of the South, saying he wanted to establish the Dudley and Pearl Fort Endowed Scholarship for deserving university students. Initially funded with 300 shares of Intel stock, Fort said the balance of the corpus would come from the proceeds of the trust he established in 1973 that was administered by the Third National Bank as well as from a percentage of the distribution from another trust. Dudley wrote that he wanted the income to go to students from Robertson and Davidson counties and for the university to award four scholarships each year, one for a member of each undergraduate class. To maintain the scholarships, Uncle Dudley recommended that the recipients maintain a 2.75 grade point average. The charitable lead trust was officially established March 3, 1994. Richard A. Johnson, the trustee, wrote the university that he intended to transfer $15,311 in 1994 "and $18,373 for the tax years required under the terms of the trust." He said that the trust was to honor Priscilla Fort, Dudley's daughter-in-law and the wife of Dr. Dudley C. Fort Jr. [25]

When Dudley C. Fort died of complications from pancreatic cancer on November 18, 1994, he left funds to the University of the South, designated for the school's summer music program. Uncle Dudley loved Shakespeare, his hot toddy, golf, his family, and friends—who were many—and the University of the South.

Chapter 5

Mildred Joy Cowan Gulbenk
1925–2008

M ildred Gulbenk was outgoing, fascinating, and different. Every single day of her life.

Born Mildred Cowan on June 12, 1925, in Nashville, Mildred was one of three children of Thomas Harvey and Margaret McGinnis Joy. She grew up riding horses on the family's large estate and nursery in East Nashville. Along with her sister Monica and her brother Tom, Mildred attended Peabody Demonstration School. There she enjoyed art and disliked math. Once, when asked in an art class to draw her dream house, Mildred drew a castle. Mildred went on to Ward-Belmont Preparatory School and Ward-Belmont Conservatory, where she majored in voice. She then studied at the Juilliard Opera School in New York.

During her adult life, Mildred was a founding member of St. George's Episcopal Church and served in its first choir. She was also an ordained priest of the Apostolic Catholic Church of Antioch. An Anglophile, Mildred visited England more than fifty times, and often conducted tours there. On these and other occasions, she spoke on English history, its historic homes and gardens, and its cathedrals. She entertained many famous people in her home, including Lady Margaret Thatcher, and was entertained by Lady Thatcher in the House of Commons. When Lady Thatcher had

From left to right, Roupen M. Gulbenk, Lady Margaret Thatcher, and Mildred Gulbenk at the Belle Meade Country Club. Photo courtesy of Roupen M. Gulbenk

dinner with Mildred and Donald, Mildred asked her if there was anyone in Nashville whom she would like to invite. Lady Thatcher said she would enjoy sharing the evening with Minnie Pearl. So, Mildred called Minnie, who was pleased to accept.[1]

Active in fulfilling her civic responsibilities, Mildred served two terms each as president of Belle Meade Plantation and Belmont Mansion, and was president of the Friends of Cumberland Heights. She donated many hours to the Horticultural Society of Middle Tennessee, the Nashville Symphony, the Opera Guild, the Association for the Preservation of Tennessee Antiquities, and other community organizations.

Mildred's first husband, Donald Cowan, was an Englishman and an architect who had moved to Nashville. She thought he was going to be her knight in shining armor and would surely take her to romantic castles in Europe like the one she dreamed about when she was a girl at Peabody. It didn't turn out that way, as Donald loved to travel but seldom did so with Mildred. To say that their marriage was an unhappy one may have been an understatement. Nevertheless, they were married for thirty-seven years, and had three children: Mary Cowan, Anne Cowan Cain, and Donald Cowan Jr. Mildred's second husband, Roupen Gulbenk, thinks she stuck with Donald so long because of the children and the fact that she loved their house, Lynnmeade, designed in 1913 by Russell Hart. Donald admitted to Mildred that one reason he married her was because he figured she, as a member of an established Nashville family, would provide him entry into Nashville society.

Before William J. "Bill" Anderson Jr. died in 1963, he and Mildred were friends. This was after Bill had twice divorced his wife, the former Alice Petway, and was living at Royal Oaks Apartments, which Donald Cowan owned. Mildred often visited Bill in his penthouse apartment, sometimes accompanied by her daughter, Anne. For some reason, Mildred called her friend, the Reverend J. Paschall Davis, to talk about her friendship with Bill. The problem was that she dialed Paschall's brother by mistake. He thoroughly enjoyed listening to Mildred but said that he thought she would never stop talking.

A closer friend of Mildred's was Dr. Mack Wayne Craig. Mildred and Mack served together on the Belle Meade Plantation board and found they had many shared interests, including travel to England, antiques, fine silver, and gardening. If Bill Anderson was a friend, Mack Wayne was a soul mate. He and Mildred traveled together to England on many occasions.[2]

While married to Donald, Mildred was a member of the Dubious Diggers Garden Club. Once, when Mildred hosted the group at her home on Lynnwood, one of the members noticed that, except for the room where the club met, all the interior doors downstairs were closed. Mildred's explanation was, "The roof leaks."[3] Once, late in their marriage, Mildred and her good friend Betty Cook Sanders had a New Year's Eve party. Mildred provided the house, and Betty paid for the party. Betty remembered in 2009 that it was so cold inside Lynnmeade that most of the ladies kept their coats on. Betty figured Donald had put the thermostat down in the low sixties. Donald denies this. Once Mildred jokingly told Betty that the allowance Donald gave her was so tight she couldn't afford to buy soap and toilet paper at Kroger at the same time.

———————⊃◦◦◦⊂———————

In the 1960s, Mildred studied spiritual healing at Findhorn, Scotland, where she met Lord Mountbatten and other aristocratic English leaders. Over the following several decades, a number of people in Nashville, including Betty Cook Sanders, experienced her powers of healing.[4] Also during the 1960s, Mildred attended a seminar on fine arts in Scotland. Larry Ray, a professor of fine arts at Lambuth College in Jackson, Tennessee, was also registered. When he saw Mildred's name and hometown on the registration list, Ray made it a point to meet her. He found her to be "a loving person, totally unique," with exuberance for life and honesty. They became good friends, traveling all over the world together many times during the 1960s and 1970s. Larry's favorite story about Mildred took place in Cairo on a trip they made soon after Egypt opened up to Western tourists. When they arrived at the Cairo airport, Larry and Mildred noticed the building was in bad shape, with bullet holes clearly visible. Nevertheless, they cleared customs and got on a tour bus to the hotel. Halfway to town, the bus stopped, and an Egyptian who obviously knew the guide came on board. He introduced himself as Faud, and inveigled the group, for a seemingly reasonable price, to take a moonlight ride in a sail-boat down the Nile that very evening. As their hotel was on the river, Faud said he would meet them in the lobby and personally escort them to the sailboat. The group, excited about a romantic, moonlight ride, accepted. That evening, after dinner, they met Faud in the lobby and followed him down, through bulrushes and some mud, to the riverbank. There, they saw two filthy oarsmen in a beat-up looking felucca. In their hostess gowns, the ladies reluc-tantly clambered aboard, followed by the equally disillusioned men. As there was no wind, the oarsmen pushed against the mud mightily with their poles but made very little progress in getting into the current. Unable to escape or even communicate with the two Egyptians, the group sat there stone-faced. Not far from the bank, one of the oarsmen broke his pole. This was followed by a lot of cussing and hollering in Arabic for someone on shore to bring another pole. Finally, someone did and, after two hours, they managed to get in the middle of the river. Still with little wind, the group spent the next two hours getting back. Mildred expressed the anger and frustration of everyone when she stood up in the middle of the Nile and said, "God damn it, I've heard of being up a creek without a paddle, but this is the worst." When they finally reached the "Promised Land," the two oarsmen disappeared, and Faud was not to be seen. For the rest if the trip, Mildred referred to Faud as "Fraud."[5]

Once, when Larry visited Mildred at Lynnmeade, he got up in the middle of the night to go to the bathroom. In the hall he met a woman he did not know. When he introduced himself, she replied that she was a "White Witch." The next morning, the "White Witch" was not to be seen.

Larry, who was extremely fond of Mildred, said that on their trips together, she talked to him a great deal about the spirit world, ghost busters, and her belief that she had been reincarnated. Larry told Mildred that her maiden name of Joy was appropriate because she loved life and was so full of joy. Larry was right. Mildred loved to share her joy with others. Having grown up around flowers at her father's nursery and later at Joy's Flowers, she enjoyed and was skilled at arranging flowers. She would often take flower arrangements to loved ones, to people in need, and to many organizations. One day, after putting as many flowers as she could in her car, she drove home without being able to see out of her rear view mirror. Mildred said to herself, "If I have a wreck on the way and kill myself, they won't have to order flowers."[6]

When Donald and Mildred's children were in Ensworth School, Mildred and Carole Nelson had a hook-up as the two families lived within a few blocks of each other. When Mildred drove, she routinely spoke to her spirit "Benji." One day, when one of the Nelson children couldn't shut the car door, Mildred shouted, "Benji, let go." The door was then easily shut. The Cowan children took "Benji" in stride, but the Nelson children were wide-eyed. Maybe Benji was to Mildred as "Harvey" was to Elwood P. Dowd (Jimmy Stewart).

After Walter Sharp died in 1973, Mildred called his niece, Ann Street, to say that she had been in contact with Walter since his death and that he wanted to talk to Huldah. Ann wisely decided not to tell Huldah. Had Huldah met with Mildred to make some spiritual contact with Walter, she would have sat across from Mildred at a table in a dark room. Mildred claimed that, when she was able to make contact, the table would shake.

One evening, Mildred called Eugenia Moore and asked her to come over "right away," that John Wisner, a former Nashvillian who worked for William F. Buckley's *National Review*, was in town staying at her house, and that she was going to make contact with his recently deceased wife. Eugenia went over to Lynnmeade and remembers that the three of them sat in the sun room around a table with a Ouija board on it. Mildred made contact with the woman and posed the question John wanted answered. It was, "What do you want me to do with all the antiques and artifacts that your parents brought back from China and left you?" Well, the Ouija board began to shake and move and spelled out the words, "Give them to Mildred." Of course, Mildred had her hands on the Ouija board but there was really not enough light for Eugenia to see if any manipulation was going on.[7]

At a party in December 1975, Donald Cowan met Bitsy Riegle. She asked Donald what he was doing. He told her that he was starting an outpatient surgery center called Parkside Surgery Center, located at Twenty-third Avenue North and Charlotte. Bitsy was intrigued with the idea and she and Donald ended up going into business together, operating out of his basement at Lynnmeade. Bitsy was there every working day. Having another woman in her house all the time naturally got on Mildred's nerves. Bitsy treated Donald with deference. For example, when they would occasionally drive to Jackson, Tennessee, where they had a second surgery center, Bitsy would drive while Donald would sit in the back seat enjoying hot coffee and Danish pastries that Bitsy provided. Once, while driving on Interstate 40 to Jackson, a tire blew out. Bitsy doesn't think there was anything suspicious about the blowout. There was some thought, however, that Mildred, not happy with having another woman in the house, had put a hex on them. In time, Donald and Bitsy sold the surgery center for a handsome profit.

Because of her strained marriage and love of travel, Mildred formed a very exclusive club named the Housewives' Club. There were only three members: Mildred, Jeanne Dudley Smith, and Georgia Twitty Chellman, who with her husband Chuck owned Veeson International Travel. The club met for lunch, usually on Sundays, and had a number of wild rules that Mildred had concocted. Members must:

1. be married and living with their husbands (but not in a perfect marriage);
2. have several children;
3. covet jewels and own a handsome collection;
4. have a spiritually open mind;
5. belong to one or more churches;

6. collect highly important and very interesting things;
7. appear on TV/radio quite often (be famous);
8. be willing to go to any place in the world on immediate notice when called upon to do so by the other two members.

Additionally, any change in personal status would result in a regular member being demoted to an auxiliary membership. This happened to Betty Cook Sanders because Mildred decided Betty's marriage was too harmonious. No wonder so few members made the cut. Jeanne Dudley Smith remembers well when they flew to Hong Kong for lunch on amazingly short notice.

When Mildred and Donald, after several separations, finally divorced, the affair was contentious. During the court action, Donald's attorney, Maclin Davis Jr., tried to portray Mildred as sort of "kooky." While interrogating her, he asked, "Do you believe in ghosts?" Mildred answered, "No." Later, Mildred's attorney, John Holland, asked Donald if he believed in ghosts. He said he once saw the ghost of Mildred's mother. This, of course, blew Maclin's strategy. After years of being on a very tight budget, Mildred got a $3 million settlement. So pleased was she with her new freedom and some money, she stopped by a pawnbroker's store on Broadway and bought a ten carat square diamond ring. Later, at the Nashville Symphony, Donald saw Mildred and noticed the large diamond ring. He asked, "Where did you get the money for that diamond?" She answered, "From you." Not satisfied, Mildred also went down to Crest Cadillac and bought a new Cadillac, a luxury car she had always wanted but never had.

In 1985, Mildred was invited to join SMOTJ (Sovereign Military Order of the Temple of Jerusalem) by Sir Gordon Sell and Sir James Hamilton, knights in this international charitable group. She was their first female member. A priest came to Nashville from New York to ordain her. The ceremony took place in Betty Cook Sanders' home by her indoor pool.

Mildred's spirit Benji, who supposedly lived in Mildred's car, was still very much around when Mildred met Roupen Gulbenk after her divorce from Cowan. One evening, while riding on a bus

Two of Mildred's business cards, courtesy of Roupen M. Gulbenk.

from the Centennial Club to the Tennessee Performing Arts Center in the early 1990s, Mildred sat immediately behind Grace (Mrs. Paul) Stumb. Grace happened to mention Roupen Gulbenk, who was a friend of hers. Mildred decided to look him up. As a starter, she drove out to his Cinnamon Hill Antique Shop on Highway 100 to ask him to appraise some silver. Soon, she was headed there every day with a sandwich and wine for lunch. Roupen and Mildred found common interests and began dating, often going to TPAC. Roupen soon learned about Benji because Mildred talked to him regularly. Roupen didn't believe in Benji but found reason to take him more seriously before long.

One night, when Mildred and Roupen were a little late going to TPAC, Mildred asked Benji to make sure they found a parking place on Deaderick Street near the TPAC entrance. Just as Roupen turned off Sixth Avenue North on Deaderick at TPAC, he noticed a car pulling out of a parking spot on the south side of Deaderick, only yards from the TPAC entrance. On a number of other occasions, Benji came through when Mildred needed something. "Benji seems to do it every time," Roupen thought to himself. Mildred either believed in Benji or put on a good act.

Grace Stumb loved Mildred and found her fascinating. Once, at a garden club meeting, Mildred told Grace that, if she would promise not to laugh, she would confide in her. Grace agreed, and Mildred told her that, in a previous life, she had been a servant at the Last Supper. Mrs. Stumb was astonished. Roupen told me in 2009 that Mildred only casually mentioned to him that she had an earlier life and never mentioned being in the room when Christ predicted that one of his disciples would betray him. A good friend of Mildred's, Eugenia Moore, remembers Mildred having told her the same story.

Once, a bearded priest named Father Stephens from New York held a Lenten service at St. George's. Mildred thought he was incredible, the real thing. He wore a hooded cassock with a rope belt and sandals. When she learned he was going to listen to confessions at a certain time, she showed up with Eugenia Moore in tow. Reluctantly, Eugenia agreed to confess her sins to the priest after Mildred did so first. After a few minutes in the booth, Mildred came out with a pained expression on her face. She said to Eugenia, "Let's go." Eugenia said, "But I haven't confessed." Mildred cut her short by saying, "He told me he held confessionals to hear sins, not sob stories."[8]

A spectacular example of Benji's mysterious power came when Roupen and Mildred went to a midnight Christmas service at St. Paul's Cathedral in London. When the service was over, about 1 AM, Mildred asked Benji to find them a cab. As the crowd poured out of the cathedral onto an otherwise dark and empty street, Mildred and Roupen crossed the street and walked only a few yards when a Mercedes pulled to a stop beside them. A dwarf in a pink suit who was driving the car asked, "Are you looking for a ride?" They said yes, and he said, "Get in." They did, although they realized they were not in a cab. When they reached the Savoy Hotel, where they were staying, Roupen offered to pay the man. He refused payment and only asked Roupen to do a good deed for someone else when he had the opportunity. From then on, Roupen, a faithful member of First Baptist Church, admitted he "three-fourths of the way" believed that Benji was real."

Roupen and Mildred married in 1993 at First Baptist Church. Because they both had prenuptial agreements, the priest at St. George's Episcopal declined to marry them, a sizeable disappointment to Mildred.[9]

By the time Roupen married Mildred, she was well known for her spiritual beliefs and was called the "Ghost Buster of Nashville." She and television personality Teddy Bart, who was also interested in the spirit world, were naturally kindred spirits; they respected each other. One day, a woman telephoned Teddy Bart to tell him that since her sister's death, a mysterious silver light, big as a refrigerator, was appearing in her bedroom every night. She asked Bart what the light meant, thinking it might be her deceased sister trying to contact her. Bart turned to Mildred for help. She promised to go out to the woman's home but one thing and another prevented her from doing so. Finally, she asked Benji or Father Andrew, another spirit friend of Mildred's, to take care of the matter. The next morning, Mildred got a call from the woman's niece, who had spent the previous night with her aunt. That night, they had seen a beautiful gold light in the bedroom at 11 PM Suddenly, they heard a voice say, "Come on over." The woman, convinced that it was her sister, answered, "No, not yet." Grateful that the mystery was solved, the two ladies called Mildred to ask if she had anything to do with the resolution. Mildred was pleased that her spirit friend had risen to the occasion.

Mildred always had a disclaimer when she made spiritual connections with the dead. She would say, "No charge and no guarantee." Actually, Mildred did more cleansings than she did séances. When Irby Simpkins and his wife moved to their new home on Hillsboro Road, Irby invited Mildred and Roupen to have dinner and asked Mildred to spiritually cleanse the house. Using words from the Episcopal Book of Common Prayer almost

Mildred Gulbenk smelling roses. Photo courtesy of Anne Cowan Cain.

verbatim, Mildred cleansed every room in the house. Roupen said, "It took all evening."

Roupen and Mildred were married for thirteen years. They traveled extensively, logging over 186,000 miles. They frequently went to Europe, even having Christmas dinner at the House of Lords. That came about as a result of James Humes, one of America's most popular platform speakers, coming to Nashville to speak at the Centennial Club and to the English-Speaking Union. On that occasion, he was a houseguest of the Gulbenks. When they casually mentioned they were going to London for Christmas, he got on the phone at Roupen's desk and called his friend Baron Crathorne and said, "Jimmy, I'm in Nashville, Tennessee, staying with my friends, Mildred and Roupen Gulbenk. They're coming to London for Christmas. Will you entertain them?" A week or so later, the Gulbenks received in the mail a parchment invitation from Lord Crathorne inviting them to the yuletide event. [10]

Another year, Mildred and Roupen had Christmas Eve dinner at Clivedon, the historic English manor house. They sat at a table with John R. Neal of Columbia and his girlfriend Cathy Clay, as well as Bradford and Jane Hooker. Roupen called it the "Tennessee table." Bradford, a philosophy professor at the University of Reading, had walked over to Roupen and Mildred's table earlier that evening and asked if they were from Nashville, having detected their Middle Tennessee accents. When they said "yes," Bradford explained that he was Henry and Alice Hooker's son.

Mildred and Roupen also visited the Caribbean and went through the Panama Canal. Each year on Roupen's birthday, Mildred would write him a letter although she never gave them to him. After her death on July 6, 2008, Roupen discovered the letters. He found them very touching and was assured by the letters that Mildred loved him despite the fact that he occasionally lost his temper and tended to be possessive of her.

In December 2008, less than six months after Mildred's death, Roupen married Bitsy Riegle, Donald Cowan's former business partner. The marriage took place at Phillips-Robinson Funeral Home, Bitsy's family business. Isn't it curious how lives get intertwined?

Chapter 6

Elizabeth Patton "Betsy" Howe
1914–1983

Despite Betsy Howe's assertions to my mother, I didn't go to bed with her. It was, on the contrary, a noble visit. It was a Sunday afternoon in 1983, and my wife Irene and I had called on Betsy at Washington Hall. I was there, in truth, to try to convince her to rejoin The Downtown Presbyterian Church, from which she had removed her membership because, as she said, "I'm not going to be dictated to by men."

She was in her final illness then, and received us in her bedroom as she was in bed. She first asked me to pour drinks from a huge bottle of whiskey that was on a swivel, and after I did that, she invited me to sit beside her. Irene and I both did, and then I made my pitch. Betsy was unmoved from her earlier decision regarding the church. Nevertheless, she was in a talkative mood and we settled back to listen.

The stories that day were about how Betsy had been kidnapped by gypsies while a child. Back then, she said, "Gypsies returned to Nashville annually to bury their dead on Murfreesboro Road." Her father went to their leader and got Betsy back only after he promised that they could visit her every year. Betsy also explained that the lines on her palm were different from that of all her friends but similar to the lines on the palms of gypsies. She held out the palm of her hand so we could see what she was talking about. That was her proof that she was a gypsy, Betsy continued. Years later, she said, when she was in Switzerland headed for France, a gypsy came up to her in a train station and told her, "You are one of us." He convinced her to change her travel plans and go with him to Vienna. Betsy also told us that she was descended from Joseph of Arimathea, the man who provided the tomb for the body of Jesus. That afternoon, she casually called Jesus "Cousin Jesus."

That was just Betsy.

———⊃⊙∘⊙⊂———

Elizabeth Patton "Betsy" Howe was the daughter of Mr. and Mrs. John Bond Atkinson Howe of Nashville. Mr. and Mrs. Howe were married November 7, 1906; she was the former Laura Brannin Barbour of Louisville, Kentucky. Mr. Howe, a native of Hopkinsville, Kentucky, came to Nashville as a boy. He attended Nashville public schools and graduated from Vanderbilt University. Shortly thereafter, he became associated with his father in the Howe Ice Company. When this family business was acquired by the Southern Ice Company, Mr. Howe went to Atlanta as vice president and general manager of the company's Georgia plant. Their oldest daughter, Barbour, was born in Nashville in 1912, before they moved to Georgia. Elizabeth "Betsy" and William H. "Billy" were born in Atlanta in 1914 and 1916, respectively. The Howes next moved to San Diego, California, in 1917, where Mr. Howe served as special food administrator under Herbert Hoover. The Howes' youngest child, Ann, was born there in 1918.[1]

Later that year, Mr. Howe returned with his family to Nashville where he founded Atlantic Ice Company, located across the street from Sulphur Dell on Fourth Avenue North. That autumn, Mr. and Mrs. Howe bought a still unfinished house on Sheppard Place that Luke Lea had begun building in 1917. The purchase price was $9,000.

In the first grade, Betsy could not speak English. She later said, "I talked German with my German nurse in the daytime, and French with my family at the dinner table. When I started to school, the teachers were upset because I knew these languages better than

English."[2] As a child, Betsy wanted to be an osteopath and a missionary. Harry Ransom, a first cousin-once-removed of Betsy's, remembered in April 2009 having visited the Howes on Sheppard Place when he was a pre-teenager and Betsy was a teenager. He was fascinated by Betsy, whom he described as "beautiful, bossy, and possessed of a strong personality."

In 1930, when Betsy was sixteen, her father built two ice manufacturing plants in Charleston, South Carolina. He called them Your Ice Company. The family, however, continued to live in Nashville. Betsy and her siblings attended Peabody Demonstration School. The Howes were members of First Presbyterian Church, and the girls each were given debut parties by their parents when they were eighteen.

Betsy and her older sister Barbour also held wild parties at their parents' home when they could. There was much drinking and some throwing of food. At one party, their first cousin, Margaret Howe, locked herself in a bathroom because she disapproved of what was going on. Margaret also remembered being in a Nashville nightclub where the young people with the Howe girls were drinking heavily.[3]

Betsy and Barbour's brother Billy was no slacker. As a teenager, he had some dates with Jean Ewing, whose mother would allow Billy to take out her daughter only if he could walk a straight line in her front hall. Jean remembered years later that Billy was daring and that he enjoyed seeing how close he could park his car to gas pumps at filling stations.[4]

Betsy told me, probably in the 1960s, that she enjoyed going swimming in the Cumberland River with her friends as a teenager. She said she once swam across the river on a dare, while her less confident and chagrined date refused to try it.

At some point, the Howes moved to Acklen, a large Victorian mansion built by Adelicia Acklen's son, Joseph Acklen, at 3300 Fairmont Drive in Acklen Park. In January 1934, when she was nineteen, Betsy made her debut at a brilliant reception given by her parents at Acklen. Over three hundred guests were present.[5] When she was a little older, Betsy tried careers in journalism and as an actress, both in Nashville and New York. Both were unsuccessful. She got in trouble in the theater because she refused to join the union. One night, she had to sneak out of a summer stock theater in

A formal pose of Betsy Howe. Photo courtesy of Ann Howe (Mrs. Robert) Hilton.

Massachusetts and make a getaway by boat. The actor Tyrone Power later delivered her luggage.

Two years after Betsy's debut, her parents gave a dinner dance at Acklen for their youngest daughter, Ann. This was Ann's formal bow to society. One hundred members of the younger generation attended. Receiving with Mr. and Mrs. Howe were the debutante's sister Barbour (Mrs. Cobb) Pilcher, Dr. Pilcher, Miss Betsy Howe, and her brother William Henry Howe. A buffet dinner was served informally preceding the dancing, for which a popular orchestra provided the music.[6]

A year or so after Ann's debut party, her father became ill. Several months later, on July 12, 1937, Mr. Howe's body was found in the Cumberland River near Shelby Park. The cause of death was drowning. John Howe was fifty-nine years old and left a widow, Laura Barbour Howe; three daughters, Barbour (Mrs. Cobb) Pilcher, Elizabeth "Betsy" Howe, and Ann Howe; a son, William Henry Howe; two sisters, Mrs. A. M. Carroll of Nashville and Mrs. Nelson Fuqua of Chicago; and a brother, William Patton Howe, of Pennington, N.J.[7] After Mr. Howe died, Betsy succeeded him as president of Your Ice Company.

The 1938 city directory shows that Betsy and Ann Howe were living at Acklen with their mother. After Ann married in 1940, Betsy and Mrs. Howe continued to live together until the latter's death on July 21, 1950.[8] In 1938, Betsy's brother Billy was living in New Jersey, and Barbour had already married. The Howes also had an African-American servant named Joseph. Harry Ransom told the author in 2009, "Sadly, Betsy treated him like a slave."[9]

———⊰∘∘∘⊱———

Barbour was an artist and a dancer, and was very dramatic. Her husband, Dr. Cobb Pilcher, was a brilliant Nashville neurological surgeon and assistant professor of Medicine at Vanderbilt.[10] Mr. and Mrs. Howe held a party or possibly a wedding reception for Barbour in the third floor ballroom of Acklen. Margaret Sloan attended. When she looked in a cubbyhole off the ballroom, she was shocked to see a nude portrait of Barbour. Margaret was satisfied Barbour was not trying to hide the painting because the door to the cubbyhole was wide open.[11]

Cobb and Barbour Pilcher had two daughters, Laura Barbour Howe Pilcher, born September 13, 1940, and Mary Dudley Pilcher, born October 5, 1942. Dr. Pilcher gained world prominence for his contributions to the field of neurosurgery. He established and developed the Division of Neurological Surgery at Vanderbilt. Dr. Pilcher died suddenly on September 22, 1949. When Barbour died in 1967, I went to the visitation to express my sadness, particularly to Betsy. I was shocked when Betsy said to me, "What do you mean sad? It was a beautiful experience!"

———⬥———

In 1939, Betsy went to Europe where she managed to get inside Germany and Austria. She even rode a German troop train into Czechoslovakia. To get out of German-occupied Europe, she successfully enlisted the help of a Russian. "I couldn't do it again, but that's the value of being young," she said. Betsy also claimed to have ridden the German rigid airship Hindenburg that crashed at Lakehurst Naval Air Station, New Jersey, May 6, 1937.

———⬥———

Once, before the United States entered World War II, Billy, a pilot, flew over the Nashville reservoir, where he proceeded to drop flour sacks that exploded releasing thick, white clouds. This caused a sensation in the neighborhood. Asked why he did it, Billy said it was bombing practice for World War II. As another joke, Billy also wore monogrammed shirts with his initials WHH, followed by the numerals XVI. When World War II came, Billy Howe was a Navy pilot. He was killed when, in bad weather, he flew his plane into a mountain; at the time, he was stationed at Pearl Harbor.

———⬥———

Ann Howe brought stability and prestige to the family when she married Dr. Frederic Tremaine "Josh" Billings Jr., the chief resident in medicine at Vanderbilt Medical School, on February 21, 1942. Several months later, Josh left for the Southwest Pacific, where he would serve in the Johns Hopkins medical unit until his discharge at the end of the war as a lieutenant colonel. Ann learned from a Dutch flier training at Smyrna Army Airfield that Dutch fliers were allowed to take their wives with them to Australia. Ann was prepared to divorce Josh, marry the Dutchman and then divorce him and remarry Dr. Billings when she got to Australia.[12]

Ann appreciated what a great husband she had landed. Josh, a native of Pittsburgh, Pennsylvania, was educated at Choate School from which he graduated in 1929. He next attended Princeton University, where he was undergraduate council president, winner of the Pyne Prize for the best all-round student, and recipient of a Phi Beta Kappa key. Also a great athlete, Josh lettered in lacrosse, wrestling and football, serving as football captain his senior year. After graduating magna cum laude with a bachelor's degree in 1933, he went to Balliol College, University of Oxford, as a Rhodes Scholar. Josh received his bachelor's degree from Oxford in 1936 and entered Johns Hopkins School of Medicine that fall. He received his medical degree in 1938 and received postdoctoral training at Hopkins and Vanderbilt, where he was from 1939 until 1942. In 2000, Princeton University named Josh Billings the "outstanding scholar-athlete of the century." Ann and Josh had three children: Dr. Frederick T. Billings III, Ann Howe Billings Harwell Hilton and John Howe Billings.[13] When Ann Howe Billings died in 2003, Dr. Billings said, "She was bright, shining and full of tricks. She was all kinds of wonderful things."

Josh Billings, Betsy's distinguished brother-in-law, had a tense relationship with Betsy. He was frequently upset over her erratic and sometimes outrageous behavior but was too much of a gentleman to let it show, much less "blow his stack."

———⟨∞∞⟩———

Betsy had a good figure and always dressed stylishly in a successful attempt to call attention to herself. She was also, according to her cousin, Harry Ransom, "a spitting image of her mother." Despite being very attractive and engaging, Betsy never married. She always said that if she married, her husband would have to have the last name of Howe, because she was not about to change her name.

At one point in her life, probably just before or after World War II, Betsy may have come close to matrimony. She met a Dutchman who was captivated by her, visiting her once or twice in Nashville. The man might have married Betsy had he been willing to change his name to Howe.[14]

Not long after the war ended, Betsy went to Paris to visit her first cousin George Litton Howe, who was a Paris banker married to a French woman named Elise. George had spent much of his life in Paris. When World War I erupted, he dropped out of Princeton and went to France to join the French Ambulance Corps. After the war, he stayed in France until the Germans overran the country in World War II, at which time Howe and his family fled south in a rented truck with all the bank's records, barely escaping the Germans. They got to Portugal and eventually to Nashville, where they stayed before returning to Paris after the war. In Nashville, Elise Howe became friends with Jane (Mrs. Robert) Harwell. When Betsy visited the Howes in Paris after the war, she looked for other Howes in the telephone directory. She also taught George's eleven-year-old son, Robert Howe, how to offer a cigarette to a lady. She pulled out her own silver cigarette lighter and demonstrated to Robert precisely how it should be done. When Robert later visited Betsy at her Acklen Park home, she taught him how to drive in Percy Warner Park. At that time, she then drove a Packard with running boards that she inherited from her parents. The George Howes also had a daughter, who was an artist.[15]

Living at Acklen alone, Betsy enjoyed referring to herself as a farmer in the middle of Nashville. Her house sat on three acres of ground, which she maintained in excellent condition, primarily by herself. In addition, she grew avocados, bananas, and plants in her conservatory, and mushrooms on the lawn. In later years, she cut her yard riding on a mower that she drove to neighborhood parties and to the Thomas Trabues, who lived across the street. She also had a horse for a long time. It was housed in a stable in the rear of the property.[16]

For a "farmer," Betsy had an active social life. Cale Haun, who lived at Braeburn with his wife Julia Fay, told his son-in-law, Bill Cammack, that when they had dinner parties, Betsy Howe was the only guest who regularly hit their *porte-cochere* with her car.[17]

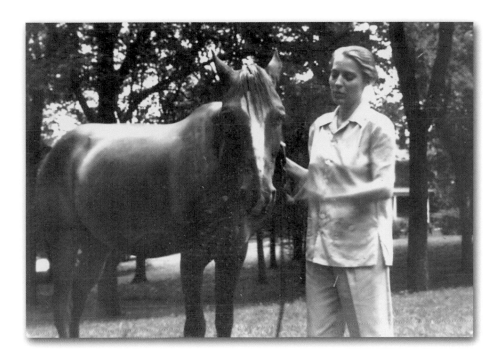

Betsy Howe with her horse. Photo courtesy of Robert L. Howe.

———◦◦◦◦———

Men seemed to like Betsy more than women did. Once, Betsy called her first cousin Margaret Howe Sloan, wife of John Sloan. When she identified herself as "Betsy," Margaret thought she was talking with Betsy Lusk. Betsy Howe told Margaret that she had a visitor from Belgium who needed a horse to ride, having been invited to participate in a Hillsboro Hounds fox hunt. In the middle of the conversation, Margaret realized that she was talking with her cousin, with whom she had little in common and whom she did not trust. Consequently, she declined to lend her horse for Betsy's friend to ride. Margaret later met the visitor, liked him and wished she had lent him the horse.[18]

———◦◦◦◦———

Once, when Tallulah Bankhead was a guest at one of Betsy's parties, Betsy supposedly climbed a tree to watch and listen to the conversations of her guests. Betsy adored her imposing house. In her own words: "I love that house. Besides, it's easier to keep a big house than a little one. If you mess up one room, just close the door and go in another one." Despite a fire that severely damaged the house one summer, Betsy simply moved to her carriage house and kept on hosting the lively parties for which she was noted. "Come have dinner with me in my Charcoal Room," she would say to her friends. "You can't stop living just because your house burns."[19]

The fire resulted in scorched walls at one end of the dining room and a charred piano. That didn't make any difference. Betsy covered the long table at the other end of the dining room with snowy linen and set on it the finest dinner service and tall tapers in silver candelabra. Asked what she had for breakfast the morning after the fire, Betsy said, "The morning the house burned, I didn't have any food so I just broiled some mushrooms on toast. What could be better?"[20]

For an evening of reading with an eclectic group of friends at Acklen and later at her home on Whitland Avenue, Betsy would select such varied subjects as a volume of the *Encyclopedia Britannica*, a best-selling novel, or an engineering manual.

Betsy attracted people like cheese attracts mice. Her friends included ministers, artists, actors, heterosexuals, homosexuals, businessmen and zoologists. She liked to mix them up at her dinner parties, which were normally black tie. "Like the British, I want to dress for dinner," she would say. Fond of men, she respected women more. "Frankly, I don't see how people put up with me," she once said. "As an ambition, I'd rather make people laugh and be happy, but my skirts seem loaded with compassion and grief. It's just as well I don't always wear trousers; skirts don't have as many pockets."[21]

Betsy also preferred adults "who communicate directly and intelligently" but admitted that, "my unorthodox old-maidenhood is full of children and animals, none of whom I particularly adore but who seem to be fond of me." She felt her worst fault was her temper. If Betsy got mad, you didn't have any trouble detecting it. Her eyes could penetrate a steel beam.

At the Iroquois Memorial Steeplechase, Betsy had a box next to one rented by Agnes "Aggie" and Livingfield More. Between races, Betsy looked at Aggie and said, "You are the artist; I am the oddest." On another occasion, Betsy was seated next to Livingfield at a formal dance at the Belle Meade Country Club. When he left the table to dance, she ate his dinner having already eaten her own.[22]

John and Fran Hardcastle were invited to one or two dinner parties that Betsy hosted. On one of those occasions, a guest commented on the inappropriateness of the new style of low-cut dresses. Betsy responded that there was nothing shocking about a little cleavage and promptly pulled out one of her breasts. John was too shocked to respond.[23] Betsy enjoyed flirting with younger men, including the Trabues' son, Tommy. He was crazy about Betsy.

Betsy's interests went far beyond hosting parties and flirting. She occasionally acted and enthusiastically supported theater, including Nashville Children's Theatre, as well as The Downtown Presbyterian Church that she had helped found in 1955.

When a majority of the members of First Presbyterian Church decided in 1954 to relocate to Oak Hill, Betsy was one of the most vociferous members in opposition to the move. Quickly, the dissenters moved to draft a trust instrument, to be known as the James I. Vance Memorial Fund, to maintain and preserve The Downtown Presbyterian Church as a place of worship. Betsy, John T. McCall and David Keeble were named to a subcommittee to draft the trust instrument. They did so in ten days and filed it with the

Acklen, home of Betsy Howe. Photo courtesy of Robert L. Howe.

Presbytery on November 26, 1954. The Presbytery denied the relief sought in the petition of the minority group, leaving the way open for the majority group to proceed with the sale of the downtown church property. After extensive negotiations, the elders of First Presbyterian agreed to sell the downtown property to a minority group that would found a new congregation, to be named The Downtown Presbyterian Church. Miss Margaret Vance of Blowing Rock, North Carolina, daughter of Dr. James I. Vance, longtime pastor of First Presbyterian Church; Walter Sharp; John K. Maddin; C. W. Kempkau; Dandridge Caldwell Jr.; and Betsy were the original trustees of the James I. Vance Memorial Fund established to preserve the one hundred and five-year-old-church building.

As a means of raising funds to purchase the old church, the James I. Vance Memorial Fund was established and trustees appointed. When The Downtown Presbyterian Church became a reality in 1955, its future was made more secure by the existence of the James I. Vance Fund, whose purpose was to preserve and promote preservation of the Presbyterian Church located at the corner of Fifth Avenue North and Church Street. In later years, whenever the James I. Vance Fund would be nearly depleted, Betsy would make contributions to keep it going. James R. "Jimmy" Cheshire III, longtime church treasurer, remembered in 2009 that when he received checks from Betsy, she would write all over the checks the various uses for which she wanted the money restricted. It was, he recalled, a nightmare to decipher what she wanted done.

At the time of the founding of The Downtown Presbyterian Church, Betsy spearheaded the production of a phonograph album *In His Shadow* as a fundraiser for the new church; she also established a Howe Trust Fund with the income designated for the physical care of the church.

Betsy was dead serious about her devotion to her church, about which she said, "I'm a non-joiner but a willing worker if I get passionate and spiritually fired up about an apparent truth of a matter or cause, and that's the way I feel about The Downtown Presbyterian Church."[24]

Once, when Betsy was helping me wrestle some concrete benches and concrete tables into place in the alley immediately east of The Downtown Presbyterian Church, she asked me what Hogan Yancey's position was on some obscure theological point. She knew I was on the pulpit committee that would soon call the Reverend Yancey to become pastor of the church. I had no idea what the point in question was, and I didn't think I could remember the question long enough to call Hogan. Consequently, I suggested to Betsy that she call Hogan if she really wanted to know.

———◦◦◦———

Betsy could be caustic at times. "I wish the Democratic Party would put up better candidates . . . that Khrushchev would get a sore throat . . . that the 'divide and conquer' idea wasn't so prevalent. . . . I'd gag on all sweetness and light, but have you ever eaten sour grapes in the dark?"[25]

———◦◦◦———

Each Halloween, when our three sons were young, The Downtown Presbyterian Church held a Halloween party with Betsy as the focal point. She always came to Fellowship Hall, where the parties were held, dressed as a witch with a floppy black hat. She did her best to scare the wits out of the children, and succeeded admirably.

When Robert E. "Rob" Harwell III was a little boy he ran into Betsy while dressed as a witch. That night, he told his father about the encounter. Mr. Harwell asked, "Was she a good witch or a bad witch?" Rob answered, "She was just a witch."[26]

Betsy liked to say, "They call me the witch of Acklen Park. One Halloween afternoon a few years ago, I was up on my roof, sweeping out the gutters. A little boy passed by on his bicycle, and asked me how I got up there. I just waved my broom at him a couple of times. He fell off his bicycle and ran away as fast as he could."

———◦◦◦———

On another occasion, Betsy was ready to bake a cake when she realized that she didn't have any eggs. Instead of driving to a supermarket, she climbed on her roof and gathered some pigeon eggs from a nest up there. Whoever ate the cake must have been surprised if they learned what its ingredients were.

With no fear of heights, Betsy even tried skydiving when that sport became fashionable in the 1960s. Unfortunately, she broke her ankle on landing, but she was, as far as she knew, the first woman in Nashville to skydive.[27]

------◦◦◦------

Betsy loved the sound of the 2,000-pound bell that Adelicia Acklen gave the former First Presbyterian Church in 1869. One New Year's Eve, when Irene and I were at home on Warner Place, I got a call from Betsy at 11 PM, asking me to drive down to The Downtown Presbyterian Church and ring that bell at midnight. Despite being reluctant to incur the displeasure of Betsy, I declined.

------◦◦◦------

Once, at a Swan Ball, Betsy misplaced her silver cigarette case (possibly the same one she demonstrated the use of to a young Robert Howe). She caused a scene, complaining that it had been stolen. Who knows?

------◦◦◦------

Betsy enjoyed having young men rent apartments in Acklen. One of them was Michael Corzine. He was there when the house caught fire and was badly damaged. He later said, "Betsy came down a fireman's ladder wearing her nightgown." One evening at a dinner party at Betsy's house, the guests were all there but no one could find Betsy. Suddenly Shade and May Murray looked up and spotted Betsy lying on a mantel dressed as Peter Pan.[28]

After the fire in the 1960s, Betsy lived for a while in her carriage house before buying Washington Hall, a striking, two-story stone house at 3700 Whitland Avenue with a recessed entrance and an octagonal dome. Built in about 1914 by Judge John Daniels, the house is reminiscent of Thomas Jefferson's Monticello. Betsy hosted many dinner parties there.

At one memorable dinner party given by Betsy at Washington Hall, her guest of honor was a well-known Northerner whom she had invited to Nashville to meet Eugene Biel-Bienne, a world-respected, Swiss-born artist who had come to Vanderbilt after World

War II to teach at Vanderbilt. Walter Sharp, head of the Department of Fine Arts and Music, was ecstatic to get Biel-Bienne, who had letters of recommendation from Picasso, Marc Chagall and other famous Parisian artists. Betsy wanted to promote Biel-Bienne and hoped that the New Yorker would take an interest in representing him in his gallery. The gallery owner, who had just been released from a New York hospital after being mugged and shot, was making his first trip to the South.

Naturally, Betsy wanted everything perfect and had instructed Ann Street, one of her guests, how she and her husband Bob should act. On the stormy and cold evening of the party, Betsy's house must have seemed like an oasis. The dining room table was elegant with a beautiful linen tablecloth adorned with her best silver and her finest crystal. In addition to the Streets, Biel-Bienne—who was known for his gruffness—and the New Yorker, Betsy had invited another Vanderbilt professor and his wife because she was particularly fond of Biel-Bienne. That lady also probably got pre-game instructions in etiquette from Betsy. The dinner party went off perfectly and Bob Street was beginning to think that he and Ann had not made a mistake in accepting.

Following dinner, just as the party was breaking up, Ann, who was entertaining the New York gallery owner in the parlor, heard a ruckus in the front hall. Fearing that something unpleasant was happening, she tried to downplay the incident to the man who was curious to find out what was happening. When he brushed by Ann and stepped into the hall, he saw Betsy and the professor's wife fighting on the floor. He exclaimed, "Oh my God, what they say about the South is true." Here is what happened: As the Vanderbilt couple and Biel-Bienne were about to leave, Betsy asked Biel-Bienne, a widower, to take home a silver platter holding the turkey left over from dinner. When he said, "No thank you" in his heavy German accent, she insisted and pushed the tray into his stomach, saying, "Take it!" At that point, the professor's wife said, "Betsy, he doesn't want it. Leave him alone." Then, the woman impulsively picked up Ann Street's purse from a chair, and hit her hostess with it. The purse flew open, spilling its contents all over the front hall rug. Dropping the silver tray holding the turkey, dressing and giblet gravy, Betsy grabbed her guest by the hair and pulled her to the floor. Bob Street, who was also in the front hall, was stunned. After a second of indecision, he leaned over and tried to pull the two antagonists apart. Meanwhile, the woman's husband, who probably didn't want to attend the party in the first place, shouted to his wife, "Get up and come home with me or don't come home at all." Thus ended the wildest dinner party Bob and Ann Street ever attended.[29]

⸺◦◦◦⸺

Once, when Harry Ransom and his wife visited Betsy at Washington Hall, they spotted her on the roof cleaning leaves out of her gutter. She had climbed up on a ladder that she usually kept propped up on the side of her house. When a friend suggested that the ladder might encourage a thief to climb it to get in the house, Betsy said she wasn't worried as she had sawed three of the rungs nearly through and knew which ones they were.

Such antics as climbing on the roof were not surprising to Betsy's next-door neighbors, George and Ophelia Paine. When they first moved there in 1976, Betsy came over to welcome them. She also wanted them to know that the stone wall separating their yard from hers, as well as part of their driveway, were on her property. As an attorney, George naturally looked at the survey he had made when he and Ophelia bought the house. He found Betsy's assertion to be false and told her so. This in no way satisfied Betsy, who then took the position that, over the years, the driveway and the wall had drifted into their yard. George fended Betsy off for some time. Then she told him that she was going to sue him to establish her right to part of his property. George answered, "Go ahead. That's how I make my living. I would welcome a legal resolution, but I must warn you, it will be expensive." George heard nothing more until one Valentine's Day, when he discovered a page from a legal yellow pad in his mail box with hearts drawn all over it. Betsy had also written on the sheet a lease agreement she had signed saying that she would lease the wall and driveway to the Paines for one dollar a year, renewable annually. While George conceded that it certainly seemed to be as reasonable an offer as anyone could expect to rent part of their own property, he declined her kind Valentine offer. The property dispute only came up in the ensuing years when Betsy was imbibing, which grew more frequent as she grew older. Ophelia and George accepted the challenges of living next door to Betsy. "It was not always easy," George wrote me in 2009, "but it was never dull. She was very kind to me. When our first son, Carter, was born, she gave me a cigar wrapped in a blue ribbon."[30]

On another occasion, when Betsy was in a reflective mood, she mused, "I wish I could be useful here on earth, but I can't help enjoying flying kites, climbing trees, and riding horses."

Betsy leased rooms in the basement of Washington Hall to young men just as she had done at Acklen. The renters had to sign agreements that they would not drink, have noisy parties, smoke, etc. Of course, these rules didn't apply to her.

Not long before her death, Betsy was in Parkview Hospital. Displeased with the food, she got out of bed one night and, in her nightgown, walked up Twenty-fifth Avenue North to Kobe Steak House, where she enjoyed a steak dinner before returning to the hospital.

When Betsy was dying of cancer at her home, Washington Hall, her young cousin, William Ransom of Atlanta, a concert pianist at Emory University, came to visit her. Betsy asked him to play "Fur Elise" by Ludwig van Beethoven on her piano in a nearby room. He did so and, after finishing, came back to Betsy's bedroom to find her dead. Uncertain what to do, he called Betsy's brother-in-law, Dr. Josh Billings, who relieved him of responsibilities.[31]

At the memorial service for Betsy in Washington Hall—which she had planned—waiters passed glasses of champagne and trays of fresh strawberries while a musician friend provided background music on the piano. Finally, the group sat down to hear the Reverend Bill Gray, the former minister of The Downtown Presbyterian Church, begin his remarks by admitting, "Betsy was difficult." There was almost a collective sigh in the room because everyone there knew that was the truth. Gray then went on to "describe and celebrate all the complexity, the humanity, the strengths, and peculiarities of a most unusual woman."[32]

Chapter 7

Andrew Lytle
1902–1995

Back in 1994, I wrote a long paper on the private boys' schools that once were so educationally important to Middle Tennessee. I planned to read the paper at two literary clubs to which I belonged: The Coffee House Club and The Roundtable. So I called Andrew Lytle, one of the South's most prominent literary figures as well as my friend, and asked if I might mail the manuscript to him for his review and suggestions. Andrew graciously said he would be pleased to read the article. Some weeks or months later, after I confirmed that he had read the paper, I drove to Monteagle to discuss it with him. When I approached the front door of Andrew's log cabin home, I immediately caught the aroma of turnip greens with "a luscious piece of fat meat" he was cooking in the kitchen. Andrew loved turnip greens or "sallet" all his life. In his essay "The Hind Tit," he wrote, "It has the appearance of spinach; but, unlike this insipid slime, sallet has character, like the life of a farmer at the head of a table. The most important part of this dish is its juice, the pot licker, a rich green liquid, indescribable except as a 'pot-licker green.' Mixed with corn bread, it has no equal." Andrew offered me some turnip greens, but I declined.

We then enjoyed a short visit before he said, "Ridley, you can write pretty well." He had not really edited what I wrote, but then offered a directive that caught me off guard. He said, "Ridley, what you really ought to do is to make the argument in your paper that we abolish the public school system. Hell, they are killing children in our schools. I'm too old to do this but you can." With that unexpected advice, I soon left and drove back to my home in Williamson County. On the way, I reflected on the point that I had been too late in asking Andrew for editorial assistance, but was, nevertheless, glad that I made the visit.

<hr />

Andrew Lytle was born in Murfreesboro, Tennessee, on December 26, 1902. His parents were Robert "Bob" Logan Lytle and Lillie Belle Nelson Lytle, both from established Middle Tennessee families. One of Andrew's ancestors founded Murfreesboro. Bob Lytle was a cotton farmer, who also harvested timber off his land, and ran a sawmill. He was also a celebrated raconteur, who made sure that Andrew learned to cherish his Southern heritage. Andrew grew up in Murfreesboro in an old-fashioned brick dwelling, two stories high with porches, held up by four square columns on each floor. He also spent time on his father's 2,000-acre cotton farm, Cornsilk, six miles out of Guntersville, Alabama. But he wasn't there a great deal until after his mother's death, because she preferred Murfreesboro.

In 1907, when Andrew was five years old, his father bought the log cabin at the Monteagle Sunday School Assembly where Andrew would spend most of his life. "At the time, Andrew was primarily interested in playing cowboys and Indians and putting on circuses under tow sack tents."[1] His mother was a Christian but not pious. She loved house parties and gaiety, and she was completely fearless in her opinion and actions. Andrew had a little sister, Polly, who was born in the front west room of the log cabin at Monteagle. Mrs. Lytle had such a difficult childbirth with Polly that a neighbor had straw put down in front of the Lytle cottage to muffle the sound of the wagons. Each June, the Lytles made the trek to Monteagle on the train from Murfreesboro. Mrs. Lytle brought with them plenty of help: a cook, a washerwoman and a nurse, all of them African-Americans. Mr. Lytle did not come regularly as he was too busy to take vacations.

One childhood story Andrew liked to tell was the time he dropped a quarter in the collection plate at church. His father noticed and pulled the quarter out and returned it to little Andrew, saying, "A penny makes just as much noise."

Andrew graduated from Sewanee Military Academy and then spent a year in France, where he was tutored. He planned to matriculate at Oxford, but the death of his grandfather caused Andrew to come home. He then entered Vanderbilt University, where he studied under English professors John Crowe Ransom and Donald Davidson—who once gave Andrew a "C,"—and philosophy professor Herbert Sanborn. Andrew also became a friend of fellow undergraduate Robert Penn Warren. Although Andrew had one poem published in *The Fugitive* magazine, he was not a member of the famous Fugitive group of poets that included Ransom, Davidson and Warren. While in Vanderbilt and for several years thereafter, his career focus was on making the theater his life's work. After graduating from Vanderbilt in 1925, he managed the Cornsilk farm for a year. Andrew then left the South to pursue his theatrical career at the Yale School of Drama where he spent two years studying to become a playwright under George Pierce Baker. He then tried professional acting in New York for a year or two.

One of the things he learned at Yale and in New York was that, to be successful as a playwright, he had to "disavow or satirize anything that was particularly Southern." Not willing to "cut himself off from his place of nativity and become a New Yorker," Lytle returned to his native South as a protest against New York and what he felt it stood for. In February 1929, while still in New York, Lytle wrote Donald Davidson at Vanderbilt to tell him "that this barbaric city is no place for a Christian to spend too much time in," and that he was coming home to research and write a biography of Nathan Bedford Forrest, whom Lytle admired above all the Confederate greats. In June, when Lytle was back in Murfreesboro, Davidson wrote to invite him to participate in a project that became *I'll Take My Stand*. Davidson, who had already signed up Ransom, Allen Tate, John D. Wade and Stark Young, said the general theme of the book would be to hold the fort against "progress." Andrew, who was by then already well into writing his first book, *Bedford Forrest and His Critter Company*, enthusiastically agreed to join in

the effort, as he too believed that the South should reject industri-
alization and cling to its rural identity. He wrote "The Hind Tit," one
of twelve essays in *I'll Take My Stand,* published in 1930 to both
acclaim and condemnation. The point of Andrew's title was to
remind a national audience that the South economically was
"sucking the hind tit and was the runt pig in the nation's litter." As
he wrote in "The Hind Tit," "the triumph of industry, commerce,
and trade, brings misfortune to those who live on the land."

Andrew continued to work on *Bedford Forrest and His Critter
Company.* To Andrew, Forrest was a heroic symbol of the Old
South—the South that H. L. Mencken had so brutally ridiculed
while covering the famed Scopes Trial in Dayton, Tennessee, in the
summer of 1925. Andrew was aware that Herbert Sanborn, his
professor at Vanderbilt, viewed the zoo-like atmosphere at Dayton
as a clash between forces for "a secular religion based on belief in
science and a spiritual religion based on faith in the Bible." Like
Sanborn, Lytle was certain the Northern diatribes were doing their
best to make the South "laughable as backward and ignorant."[2]

Everything Andrew learned from growing up in Murfreesboro and
at Cornsilk told him that the South was not as backward as the
"modernists" would have the whole world believe. He was now
fighting back and, with the counsel of Frank Owsley, an older friend
and noted historian, Andrew would write three novels in the 1930s
and 1940s to make his Agrarian statements. They were *The Long
Night* (1936), *At the Moon's Inn* (1941) and *A Name for Evil* (1947).
Andrew wrote most of *The Long Night* at Cornsilk. Stripped to his
shorts, he would carry his typewriter to his favorite log on a hill
behind the house and spend the day writing. Later, Andrew wrote
The Velvet Horn (1957), which critics would consider his master-
piece; *The Hero with the Private Parts* (1966); *A Novel, A Novella and
Four Stories* (1958); and *A Wake for the Living* (1975). The last was a
history of the land and what man had done with it and to it. The book
is also a history of people and the societies that shaped them. *The
Hero with the Private Parts* is a collection of Andrew's essays.

Andrew first lived year-round in the Assembly during the Great
Depression, when he and his wife Edna, not long married and short
of funds, lived in the log cabin for a couple of years. Andrew
remembered that snow drifted into the halls and one winter, a

From left to right, Caroline Gordon (Mrs. Allen) Tate, Anne Goodwin Windslow, Andrew Lytle, Edna (Mrs. Andrew) Lytle, Nancy Tate (daughter of Allen and Caroline Gardon Tate), Allen Tate, Robert Lowell, and Jean Stafford at Monteagle, Tennessee in 1943. Photo courtesy of the Monteagle Sunday School Assembly archives.

bucket of water froze in front of their bedroom fire. Except for winter, the days were pleasant and Andrew saw a great deal of students and old friends from Sewanee. Andrew won a Guggenheim Fellowship[3] that spared them a third winter in the log cabin. On his return, the University of the South's vice chancellor offered Andrew a house on the domain rent free if he would agree to give two public lectures. For a number of reasons, including the fact that his log cabin roof leaked and the Monteagle Assembly was lonely in the wintertime, Andrew accepted. While living in Sewanee, his oldest daughter, Pamela, was born.

Andrew's friends Allen Tate and Caroline Gordon and their daughter Nancy also lived in the Assembly during the 1930s. At various times, the Tates rented the Wallace, Donelson, and Dalrymple cottages. They lived with Andrew one entire winter; Caroline is said to have fallen though the porch at Andrew's log cabin while pregnant.

In the late 1930s, while still living at Sewanee, Andrew went bird hunting with Sinclair Buntin at one of the Buntin farms in Robertson County. Shade Murray and two of Elizabeth Buntin's younger sons were there. That night, at Elizabeth's lovely old house, where they had dinner, Louie and Betty Phillips and Hester Buntin Gale and her husband George were also guests. The entertainment that evening was disagreements between Elizabeth and her boys. Mrs. Buntin told Andrew about the old Stringer farm being for sale seven miles away. Andrew, who wanted to farm on good land, bought it and he and Edna began fixing up the place in 1939. Andrew renamed the home Cornsilk after his father's plantation near Guntersville, Alabama. A typical mid-nineteenth century Tennessee farmhouse, the old house was two stories tall with a distinctive, recessed two-story front porch. Built of yellow poplar, it was still sound even though tenants had lived in it for thirty years. Lytle added a one-story wing but carefully preserved the house's original architecture.[4] There were no fences, and the cistern didn't work. The farm had a racetrack, two tenant houses, three tobacco barns, a log barn, a stock barn and a schoolhouse, where Andrew raised turkeys. He also brought from Sewanee one hundred and forty chickens that he had raised in his garage on the mountain. Andrew had a chicken house built for them.[5] Having the farm with deep soil, Andrew relished walking barefoot in plowed fields and his garden. In truth, however, he was a better writer and storyteller than farmer.

When The University of the South invited Andrew to join the English department in 1942, he accepted. With gasoline rationing, he could function better at Sewanee than on an isolated farm and would have congenial people of letters with whom to converse, something he did not have in rural Robertson County. He also realized how difficult it was to farm and write at the same time.[6] At Sewanee, where Allen Tate was one of his advisory editors, he edited the *Sewanee Review*, then a modest journal. Andrew taught at Sewanee until 1944. By then, he had elevated the *Sewanee Review* to be recognized as one of the nation's most prestigious literary quarterlies. He later taught at Southwestern at Memphis (now Rhodes College), Kenyon College, the University of Kentucky and Vanderbilt. He also taught two semesters at the University of Iowa as a visiting professor, in the springs of 1947 and 1948. One of his students there was Walter Sullivan, who would go on to teach English at Vanderbilt for five decades. In 1948, Andrew founded the writing program at the University of Florida. He lectured there from 1948 until 1961.

After leaving Sewanee to teach elsewhere, Andrew would visit Monteagle every summer. While there, he frequently walked over from his log cabin to Restover, the home of his next-door neighbor Irene Morgan Weaver. There, they would sit and talk. Mrs. Weaver's grand-daughter, my wife Irene, then about eight years old, remembers one such visit when Andrew was there telling stories in the living room. Her grandmother said, "Andrew, you tell even better stories than you write." As a child, Irene always thought the Lytle Cottage was haunted and that there was a ghost on the porch. Irene's best friend at Monteagle was Elizabeth Ewing, who lived in the Keeble Cottage across the street on the corner. When the two girls went to movies at night in the auditorium, they always ran by the Lytle Cottage.

In the late 1940s, when Andrew was teaching at Florida in the winter and living on his Robertson County farm in the summer, Mrs. Weaver didn't like seeing his cottage vacant most of the year. She persuaded Andrew to sell it to the MSSA Woman's Association, whose building and three other public buildings had burned in a fire earlier that year.

Andrew returned to the University of the South in 1961, where he taught English until his retirement in 1973. During this time, he reclaimed his position as editor of the *Sewanee Review*, replacing Monroe Spears, who had kept the reputation of the magazine at a very high level. Andrew's editorial success on his second tour of duty equaled that of his first from 1942 to 1944. Among the promi-nent writers whose stories were published in the *Sewanee Review* during that era were Thomas E. Adams, Harry Brewster, Harry Crews, Caroline Gordon, Madison Jones, Claude F. Koch, George

Lanning, Flannery O'Connor, Charlie Rose, Allen Tate, Eleanor Ross Taylor, Peter Taylor and Robert Penn Warren. Andrew himself published little new work after resuming the editorship of the *Sewanee Review*. As he said, "My pace of writing is generally very slow, with constant cleaning up and structural revisions. Too often, I will spend a day on a paragraph; a page is a good day's work."[7]

It was fortuitous that in 1961, the Woman's Association acquired the residence of the late Miss Ella D. Winfield, who had left her home to the Assembly. The Woman's Association then sold the log cabin it had acquired from Andrew Lytle in 1948 back to him. He would live there for the rest of his long life.

In the summer of 1961, Ann Bradford Ewing was sitting in a chair beside Andrew Lytle at a lawn party at the cottage of Arch and Deanie Dalrymple in the Assembly. Ann was very pregnant with her daughter, Christy. Andrew turned to Ann and said, "Ann, you look as virginal as ever!" Three decades later, Ann asked Andrew how he was getting along. He answered, "Oh, I'm doing all right but I notice I'm losing my countenance."

⸻◦◦◦⸻

During his twelve years teaching at Sewanee in the 1960s and 1970s, Andrew invited writers and English students to his log cabin home in Monteagle, where he would hold court on his wraparound porch in good weather and in front of a fire in cold weather. He would serve his favorite bourbon, Old Rip Van Winkle, "aged ten years in the wood," in silver cups while dispensing wisdom and charm. Andrew once told Oxford, Ohio, English professor Bill Pratt that he had a case of "Old Rip Van Winkle" stored in the basement for his wake. Among Andrew's students were many prominent writers including Flannery O'Connor, Madison Jones, Harry Crews, and Merrill Joan Gerber. Andrew was very popular with his students and continued his tradition of holding court well into his retirement years. Many of his young visitors made every possible effort to appear to be sophisticated and worldly, particularly if they came with a date. Andrew's guests were welcome company since his wife, Edna, had died in 1963, and he was lonely.

Andrew Lytle seated in the central hall of his log cabin at Monteagle, Tennessee. The portrait shown behind him is of his aunt Mary Nelson as a child. Photo from "A Literary Life" The Atlanta Journal, February 28, 1963.

When Brad Gioia, Montgomery Bell Academy's headmaster, arrived at the University of the South as a freshman in 1972, Andrew Lytle was still there. An English major, Brad remembers being "almost mesmerized by the associations Mr. Lytle had at the *Sewanee Review*, the friendships he had forged with individuals like Allen Tate, and the legendary events and travels he had made in his life journey." Gioia recalled in 2009, "Andrew Lytle practically bewitched us with his kindness, tutelage and companionship. My first encounter with him was beside a fire at his Monteagle cabin. What seemed like thirty silver goblets filled with straight bourbon surrounded me. I think it was my first drink of bourbon in a goblet of ice that evening beside the fire. Andrew Lytle took a kind interest in me and invited me regularly for lunch or dinner and conversation. Not infrequently, I would find a note in my dorm room or in my post office box with a kind invitation to be part of some celebratory affair at the Monteagle Assembly. Sometimes those notes were written on the back of an earlier draft of his last work *A Wake for the Living*. I prized those notes as some of the most special invitations and notes I had ever received. Andrew Lytle served for me—as he did for almost two generations of undergraduates—as a great uncle or grandfather on the mountain. I attribute my interest in literature, and particularly Southern literature, to the moments and friends we shared."[8]

After Irene Weaver died in 1957, her daughter and son, Henriette Weaver Jackson and William C. Weaver Jr., inherited Restover. They came to Monteagle every summer with their families and enjoyed Andrew's friendship just as much as Mrs. Weaver had. My wife and I both remember sitting on the Weaver porch with Andrew, Irene's parents, and, sometimes, one or two others, on summer afternoons, and being regaled by Andrew's stories. Robert Penn Warren once called Andrew the best conversationalist he had ever known.

In 1966, Allen Tate moved to Sewanee with his third wife, a former nun named Helen Heinz, whom he met while teaching at the University of Minnesota. In 1967, Helen gave birth to twin boys, John and Michael Tate. When the twins were eleven months old, Allen and Helen left them in the care of a babysitter while they had dinner with Andrew Lytle at his Monteagle log cabin. While they were gone, the babysitter left Michael in the playpen while she bathed John. With her out of sight, Michael choked to death on a plastic toy. For some reason that Andrew could not understand, Helen blamed him for the tragedy. As a result, Allen and Andrew were estranged until Allen's death in 1979.

On special occasions during the 1960s at Monteagle, Andrew would occasionally perform a Cossack dance, wearing heavy black boots. This took considerable agility as the Russian dance called for him to crouch and, alternatively, kick out his legs. He performed it well and impressed three generations of admirers.

Occasionally, Andrew would drive to Nashville. On a trip there to visit a friend he was seen in an elevator in a downtown high rise clutching Rosy Bell, his pet turkey, to his chest. He could also be seen walking around the Monteagle Assembly grounds followed by Rosy Bell, who slept on the footboard of his bed. Eventually, Rosy Bell fell victim to a hungry tenant farmer.[9]

Once while ambling down Boxwood Place in the Assembly after his retirement, Andrew noticed Oliver Jervis, Sewanee Class of 1958, mulching his yard. Andrew stopped to watch and asked Oliver what the machine was. Oliver told him it was a machine to mulch dead grass and leaves and return their nutrition to the soil. Andrew said nothing but simply nodded, and Oliver could tell what was going through his mind. The old Agrarian liked the idea of enriching the soil, but didn't care much for the machine.

———◦◦◦◦◦———

Some years later, when Andrew was a little unsteady on his feet, Dr. Walter Merrill accompanied Andrew, who was on his way to the mall, from his house on Walnut Avenue. Walter asked Andrew if he walked often. Andrew said, "Only when I have someplace to go."

———◦◦◦◦◦———

In 1989, Andrew attended a conference at Russell Kirk's home, Piety Hill, in Mecosta, Michigan. Mr. Kirk was an important figure in the post-World War II conservative movement and ran a salon there. Andrew's old friend, Cleanth Brooks, then living in New Haven, also attended. Andrew brought up from Tennessee a brilliant Sewanee student, Jon Meacham, whose job was to mix drinks in the evenings and make coffee in the mornings for Andrew.[10] Meacham graduated from Sewanee magna cum laude and became a Pulitzer prize-winning author and editor of *Newsweek* magazine.

Andrew was an institution at Sewanee and in the Monteagle Sunday School Assembly. Although he could not always remember everyone's name at either place, he was instinctively courteous and charming. Normally, he wore a fedora, which he tipped whenever he passed a lady while walking to the mall or on the campus. In his later years, he continued to drive his car reasonably slowly about the mountain.

Late in his life, Monteagle Assembly friends Bill and Fran Reynolds went to eat with Andrew at the Sewanee Inn. He ordered "unsweet" tea and meticulously added a sweetener and a twist of lemon. A few minutes later, their waitress came by and refilled Andrew's partially filled glass of tea. He upbraided her, saying, "You've ruined my tea. I had it exactly the way I like it." A few years earlier, in the winter of 1982, Eugene "Gene" Nelson, a French major at Sewanee, applied for admission to Vanderbilt Medical School.

Andrew Lytle in 1986. Photo courtesy of the Nashville Public Library, Special Collections.

After an initial interview, Gene did not hear from Vanderbilt. Frustrated, he asked Mr. Lytle to write a recommendation to the director of admissions. Andrew did, and, within 10 days or so, someone from the Vanderbilt admissions office got back in touch with Gene, who was given a second interview and accepted into the medical school, Class of 1987.

Andrew Lytle, an unrepentant advocate for rural Southern values and the last surviving member of the famous Agrarian literary group, died at his home in Monteagle on December 15, 1995, at age ninety-two. Assembly members remembered him for his charm, for his wonderful stories, and for the prestige he brought to the Assembly. His sister, Polly Lytle Darwin of Huntsville, Alabama; two daughters, Pamela Lytle of Sewanee and Langdon

Chamberlain of St. Andrews, Tennessee;[11] and five grandchildren, for whom he left a wonderful legacy of books and stories, survived him. Oh, one more thing, they did not serve Old Rip Van Winkle Bourbon at Andrew's visitation. There was only a small bit left in one bottle. That night, however, at the Sewanee Inn, a group of students drank bourbon to his memory.[12]

Dan May

1898–1982

W hen I am with my good friend Jack May, I almost feel that his father is also in the room. Jack had the fortune to inherit a full measure of Dan May's keen intelligence and wit. I was always impressed with the way Dan demonstrated that brainpower on the Metropolitan Council, in particular.

Dan May was born in Nashville on Christmas Day 1898. He was the youngest of three sons of Jacob and Rebecca May. Jacob May was a German immigrant who moved to Nashville from New Hampshire to establish, in 1896, the South's first hosiery mill, May Hosiery Mills. It was then located in a shop inside the Tennessee State Prison between Fifteenth Avenue North and Prison Alley. Dan May contracted with the State of Tennessee for prisoners to work in the mill. This lasted until 1897 when the State Legislature abolished the practice of private companies contracting with the state for prison labor.[1]

In 1908, when Dan May was nine years old, his father built the May Hosiery Mills plant at the corner of Fourth Avenue South and Chestnut Street. From then until the black powder plant was built at Old Hickory in 1918, May Hosiery Mill was the city's largest employer. Decades later, Dan recalled, "I grew up in the mill, working there in summer vacation until I finished college. There was no escaping it." Dan also rightfully considered his father a pioneer.

Dan was educated in Nashville public schools, graduating from Hume-Fogg High School in 1915. He entered Vanderbilt that fall in the class of 1919, and would have graduated with his class had he not enrolled in the Student Army Training Corps in 1918. While at Vanderbilt, Dan made quite an impression. He was managing editor of the *Vanderbilt Hustler*, editor-in-chief of *The Commodore*, president of the Pan-Hellenic Council, an intercollegiate debater, one of the founders of Zeta Beta Tau fraternity, and a member of the Calumet Club with future Fugitive poet Allen Tate. Two of his staff members on the *Hustler* were Ralph McGill, future editor of *The Atlanta Journal-Constitution*, and Joe Hatcher, future political columnist for *The Nashville Tennessean*. Dan graduated with a mathematics major, which led to a lifelong interest in astronomy.[2]

After graduation in 1920, Dan entered Vanderbilt Medical School. After completing one year, he dropped out as his father needed him to assume responsibility for managing Bloch Clothing Company, a poorly performing wholesale clothing business on the public square that Mr. May and a kinsman, who had just died, owned. Three years later, Dan liquidated the company in a responsible manner. While unpleasant, this proved to be a valuable learning experience for the young businessman, who then joined the family hosiery company in 1927 as treasurer.

On June 14, 1927, Rabbi Julius Mark married Dan and Dorothy Fishel of Nashville at the Vine Street Temple. Among the wisecracks that Dan's friends made about the marriage were that, "the fourteenth of June is the last of May;" "What did Dan say when he proposed to Dorothy? 'Yes;'" and "FOR SALE: One fishing outfit. 'Do not need it anymore.' Dan May."

Like her husband, Dorothy May was educated in the Nashville public schools. She attended Vanderbilt before transferring to Wellesley College, Massachusetts, where she graduated in 1925.

The same month Dan and Dorothy married, he joined a Jewish literary group, the Shamus Club, founded two months earlier. The original twelve members included Herbert Kohn, who had come to Nashville to work with the YMHA. Dan wanted to meet him, so he walked in Kohn's office in the old Young Men's Hebrew Association at 712 Union Street and said, "I'm glad to meet you Mr. Cohen."

Dan and Dorothy May at the Acropolis in Athens, Greece. Photo courtesy of Joseph "Jack" May.

Kohn replied, "'I am glad to meet you too, but my name is 'Kahn,' not 'Cohen,'" to which the irrepressible May replied "If K-o-h-n is 'Kahn,' then M-A-Y spells November." Forty-three years later, Dan remembered, "I never apologized, but will one of these days."[3]

Dan worked hard to keep May Hosiery Mills profitable during the Great Depression, when hosiery mills in the South were closing left and right, and during World War II. Between 1927 and 1945, he never took a vacation. Dan also knew the names and circumstances of all his employees and kept their best interests at heart. It was his business skills and mental sharpness, however, that caught the eye of Nashville businessmen, educators, and civic and charitable leaders who wanted him on their boards.

As a student of history, Dan watched, with growing alarm, Hitler's rise to power in Germany during the 1930s. He and his brother Mortimer saw, before nearly all Americans did, that German Jews were being persecuted terribly and that a worse fate was in store for them. He and Mortimer were responsible for getting some two hundred and ten Jews out of Germany in the years before World War II. One of them was Ernest Freudenthal, who was not quite seventeen years old when he arrived in America in 1937. The Mays had to give the U.S. Government an affidavit of support for every Jewish man and woman whom they brought to Nashville, and any refugee who wanted a job at May Hosiery Mill got one. Freudenthal, who became an outstanding Nashvillian, said, "A lot of us owe our lives to the Mays." Jacob May was a native of Germany who used many German expressions throughout his life.

During World War II, May Hosiery Mills made socks for American soldiers. In addition to his responsible position at the family business, Dan served on the war production board for fifteen months with a pay of one dollar per year. After the war, he asserted that during the World War II, he "fought the Battle of South Nashville."

Dan was promoted to manager of May Hosiery Mills in January 1946. Four years later, in May 1950, he was named chairman of the board, a position he would hold until his retirement in 1963 at the mandatory age of sixty-five.

In November 1944, Dan, then the company treasurer, was named to the city's Board of Education by Mayor Thomas L. Cummings. Dan served the remaining two years of another person's term who had resigned due to ill health. Because of his exemplary leadership, Dan was elected to a full three-year term two years later. In 1947, the Nashville Chamber of Commerce named Dan to chair the chamber's committee on education. Several years later, *The Nashville Tennessean* and the *Nashville Banner* both supported the candidacy of Dan for president of the Nashville City Board of Education. Dan won and began serving in January 1950. One of his progressive moves was to give the county school board thirty-nine unused classrooms that the city school system owned.

When Dan's term expired at the end of 1952, more than one hundred Nashvillians circulated petitions asking Mayor Ben West to reappoint him to the board. The local Parent Teacher Association unanimously advocated his reappointment as did Mrs. Luke Lea, who wrote *The Tennessean*, "It would be a great tragedy for every child in the Nashville school system if Mr. May is not allowed to continue as a member of the Board of Education." The Nashville Branch of NAACP also endorsed the reappointment of Dan May. The NAACP described him as a far-sighted and progressive leader. Needless to say, Dan was reappointed.

By 1952, Dan had been, for five years, a member of the board of Fisk University. He would continue in that role for another five years before retiring because of a philosophical difference with the president. From 1951 until 1957, Dan was on both the Fisk and Vanderbilt boards. He said he spent half his time trying to nudge the Vanderbilt board from the nineteenth into the twentieth century and the other half trying to pull the Fisk board back from the twenty-first century. Dan, who would remain a faithful member of the Vanderbilt board until his death in 1982, was one of the largest private contributors to the contents of the Joint University Library's browsing room.

⎯⎯⎯◦◦◦◦⎯⎯⎯

When Eugene Vaughan of Houston first joined the Vanderbilt Board of Trust in the 1970s, he and another new member were invited to make remarks. The other man prefaced his remarks by saying his wife told him not to talk for long. After he spoke for what seemed like twenty minutes, trustee Dan May quipped, "You should have listened to your wife."

———————

On another occasion, Dan stopped on the Vanderbilt campus to chat with a groundskeeper. This happened just after one of the university's learned educators had been granted the title of professor emeritus. The groundskeeper, who was very fond of the scholar, remarked, "He should have gotten that title twenty years ago." Dan loved it.

———————

In the eulogy delivered by Harvey Branscomb at Dan May's funeral in 1982, the retired Vanderbilt chancellor spoke of his good friend's individuality. Branscomb said, "The real basis of his uniqueness was an inner strength and independence, which enabled him to be and remain himself under all conditions and circumstances. He was not a conformist. He could not be pressured into a course he did not believe in, nor seduced by the natural desire to be agreeable. He said what he thought and stood for what he believed in. Once after he had been in a decided minority on an issue before a board on which he and I were members, he dismissed my reaction to it with the remark he often used, 'Don't forget that God and one are a majority.' He laughed when he said it, but I knew him well enough to know that it expressed his character. Dan May had moral courage. He stood for what he believed."[4]

———————

When Dan's son, my friend Joseph "Jack" May, was a teenager, one of his closest friends—Robert K. "Bob" Massie, future author of *Nicholas and Alexandria*—was often in the May home. Accordingly, he had many opportunities to listen to Mr. May, who usually got home from the hosiery mill not long after the boys got home from school, having gone to work earlier than most dads. When Mr. May first took note of Bob and his brother Kim, he said, "You're Molly Todd's boys. She's a fine woman, but, of course, her politics are dead wrong." Molly was a liberal. Dan fervently believed in capitalism and said he was "a Republican down South when it was considered an underground movement."[5]

——◦◦◦◦◦——

Another of Dan's colorful sayings with a political bent was: "Too many of America's liberals are under the mistaken impression that they have a monopoly on morality." He defined a liberal as "someone who is farther away from the situation than you are." In the 1960s or 1970s, he said, "I've always been troubled by the white 'liberals' of Nashville who were strong advocates of busing when it was a Mississippi issue, but were quick to enroll their kids in private schools when integration came to Tennessee." On another occasion, he said, "I try to be liberal without being foolish, and conservative without being reactionary." Dan's definition of an honest politician was, "one who honestly didn't know what his supporters had done to get him elected."[6]

——◦◦◦◦◦——

One of Dan's greatest pleasures was his longtime membership in the Nashville Rotary Club, which he joined in the 1950s. He remained a member until his death three decades later. In 1959, the same year Dan was made a director, film star Ronald Reagan visited the Nashville Rotary Club representing General Electric. The actor's reviews were mixed. Dan May didn't like the speech and wrote GE to complain. May wrote, "He makes a very popular kind of speech and much that he said contained truth. On the other hand, much that he said was utter rot. . . . The case for American business should be presented by intelligent men. This is not the same thing as saying it must be represented in a dull manner."[7]

——◦◦◦◦◦——

In August 1960, the year Dan was elected vice president of the Rotary Club, he spoke about a recent trip to Russia that included four days in Leningrad. May said, "Here is a country ill fed, ill clothed, and ill housed but inhabited by some 200 million people who think they have the key to the future."

Dan was elected president of the Rotary Club in 1962. In remembering that year, he said, "I don't recall anything but happiness that year. I had more ham in me than the Rabbi approved of."[8]

May always credited Rotary with enlarging his "civic scope," but the record shows that the benefit worked both ways, for May expanded—and sometimes challenged—the civic awareness of the Rotary Club. His quirky humor enlivened all he did. May often presided over Rotary luncheons while wearing a suit, tie and tennis shoes. Invariably, when fellow Rotarians asked, "How's the sock business, Dan?" he would reply, "Better than next year."

As president of the Rotary Club, Dan May was said to provide "a wonderful combination of wit and leadership." No one ever wanted to miss May's off-the-cuff comments during meetings. For example, there was his legendary assessment of a renowned economist who spoke at the club: "One day I'm going to find a one-armed economist so he can't say 'on the other hand.'" Dan also commented on starting each meeting by giving the Pledge of Allegiance: "I love the flag," Dan said, "but you'd think my pledge would be good for more than one week." And finally, his refusal of coffee with his meal: "No, thank you. It might keep me awake during the program."[9]

Dan May's introduction of *Tennessean* publisher John Seigenthaler at Rotary Club, shortly after Seigenthaler had returned from his stint with the Kennedy Administration, was classic May. After giving a brief biographical sketch of John, including where he was born, raised, educated, and entered journalism, Dan continued, "The only time Seigenthaler was away from Nashville was in the Kennedy Administration when he was gone for fifteen months. During that time he helped integrate the Deep South. Some damn fool hit him on the head with an iron pipe, and some say he's never been the same since." After a spontaneous eruption of laughter, Dan continued, "From the State Capitol you can see the statue of Edward Ward Carmack, the former editor of *The Nashville Tennessean* who was assassinated because of what he wrote in the newspaper. Many people thought Carmack got what was his due, and that the present editor deserves the same fate." By then, the Rotarians were roaring with laughter. Dan interrupted them to say, "Whatever your personal or political views, Seigenthaler has something in common with every Rotarian in this room. He shares a deep love for this city, and a deep understanding of how it should work. I present to you, the people of Nashville, someone who loves this city as you do." From that day on, John said he was accepted by the Nashville establishment.[10]

One day at a Rotary Club meeting at The Hermitage Hotel, Felix Dodd, Ken Hardcastle, and Dan were talking about integration in Nashville. Thinking that Dan was much more liberal than they were, one of them asked "Dan, would you let your daughter marry a black man?" Dan responded, "You are absolutely right. I would not. As a matter of fact, I would not want her to marry a Protestant."

Dan was program chairman of the Rotary Club in 1965 when Genesco opened its new world headquarters in Genesco Park on Murfreesboro Road. The club met there and Dan introduced the speaker, Ben Willingham, president of Genesco. In his introduction, Dan said, "Ben has been in and out of women's brassieres for nine years." Hopefully, most in the audience knew that Genesco had owned Bonwit Teller, the high-end ladies' department store, since 1956.

Three generations of Dan's family have been Nashville Rotarians: Dan, Jack, and Andrew, Jack's son.

———

In addition to serving on the Fisk, Meharry, and Vanderbilt University boards, the City Board of Education, as president of the YMHA, vice president of the Jewish Community Council (1954), and as a member of Vine Street Temple, the colorful May seemed to be everywhere in the community. He was for twelve years a magistrate, and served brilliantly on the first Metro Council, having received the most votes countywide of all the at-large candidates. Vice Mayor George Cate Jr., who presided over that first Metro Council, said, "There was not a single member of the council that was more instrumental in its success than Dan May." Decades later, Cate recalled a council meeting when Dan went into a rage that ended as suddenly as it started. Minutes later, he walked over to George and said, "I never lose my temper unintentionally."[11]

Deeply committed to the cause of public education in Nashville, Dan was a strong supporter of human rights. The first member of Nashville's Jewish community to hold many of the public positions he attained, May worked tirelessly to improve the lot of others who suffered discrimination.

In November 1954, County Judge Beverly Briley appointed magistrate Dan May to the school committee. Two months later, May said that board members who refused to take orders from City Hall under Mayor Ben West's administration couldn't expect to be reappointed. This was May's first public accusation that Mayor Ben West was tampering politically with the school system. In January 1958, hot words flew between Dan and Ewing Clouse, another magistrate who threatened a lawsuit to test the constitutionality of the one-government commission. May said, "Today's session was a disgrace and a waste of taxpayer money." Later that year, again speaking as a magistrate, Dan made the argument that "Davidson County and other Southern communities have starved their schools for years." On yet another occasion in 1958, May, chairman of the Davidson County Court's school committee, took a verbal slap at some of his colleagues who advocated lower school funds and two-shift classes. Dan said, "One of my friends in Quarterly Court drives a no-shift car yet he wants schools to run with two shifts."

In 1960, Dan May, still chairman of the school committee of the Davidson County Quarterly Court, made the motion to endorse the creation of an educational television station, Channel Two, now Channel Eight. The motion passed unanimously. Nashville has benefited enormously.

Despite his serious commitment to improving his hometown in every imaginable way, Dan continued to amuse his friends with his humor. He once said of Mortimer: "My brother has one thing I don't have: a hardworking brother." When Nashville had an eclipse of the sun, Dan said, "Viewing a total eclipse of the sun was the most exciting ninety seconds I've ever had with my clothes on." He also took gentle aim at his wife, once saying, "After several decades of marriage, I can assure you that I make all the important decisions in the family. So far there haven't been any." Dan had advice for first-time fathers, suggesting, "When your wife brings the baby home, offer to hold it, then drop it. It won't hurt the baby and your wife will never ask you to do anything with the baby again." On infidelity, he had this to say, "There was the story of the fellow who received a letter from another fellow that read, 'I resent your running around with my wife when I'm out of the city. Come to my office tomorrow at 10 AM' Fellow Number One replies, 'I received your circular letter, but I cannot attend the meeting. I'll go along with what all the others decide.'"[12]

By 1959 Dan, as a magistrate who had the confidence of Beverly Briley, did everything he could to hold Briley's feet to the fire on his support of metropolitan government. On August 24, Dan May took the floor during the quarterly court's special session to issue $2,500,000 in district county school bonds and $500,000 to build the sewage disposal system to serve the new Gates Rubber plant in Madison, Tennessee. He said, "It is almost impossible to run two governments when we need one. Due to two taxing authorities, we are overburdened with taxes." The next January, he predicted, "taxes will go up under any circumstances, as they already have, but they will go up far less under one government than under double government."

Nobody seemed to escape Dan's humor. Here are some examples. First: "There's the story of the Jewish lady who gave her husband two neckties for his birthday. The next day he came down to breakfast, proudly wearing one of his new ties. 'I knew it,' she said. 'I knew you didn't like the other one.'" The next joke may have been directed at Rabbi William "Bill" Silverman at The Temple, with whom Dan had sharp disagreements on matters of theology and economics. Dan quipped, "Tell me, Rabbi, can a Jew save money in a piggy bank?" Poking fun at his own over-commitment to civic responsibilities, Dan once said, "If, when the sun goes down, a Jew in Nashville doesn't have at least two meetings to go to, he's shirking his civic responsibility." The next joke may well have been told at Rotary. This was "the story about the fellow who was out cutting the grass one day in a ritzy Nashville suburb. The fellow had

From left to right, Barrett Sutton, Mayor Beverly Briley, and Dan May in October 1968. Photo courtesy of Joseph "Jack" May.

gotten married several years before to a very rich lady. It was a scalding hot summer afternoon, and the fellow had taken his shirt off. A policeman, who happened by, said, 'You shouldn't be out there without your shirt on. What would people think if your wife was out here cutting the grass without her shirt on?' The fellow replied, 'They would certainly know that I didn't marry her for her looks.'" Here's another good one. "A little boy was standing on the corner. He was crying and crying. A man came up to the boy and asked, 'What's the matter?' 'My mother and father are arguing all the time,' the little boy said. 'Who is your father?' the fellow inquired. 'That's what they're arguing about.'"[13]

In a jibe at his good friend John Seigenthaler, May once said, "There are always four versions of any speech I give. The first is the speech I plan to give. The second is the speech I actually give. The third is the speech I wish I had given when I get home and think about it. And the fourth is the speech I read about in *The Tennessean* the next morning."[14]

In the mid-1970s, Dan began widening his repertoire of jokes as he considered his own mortality. Here are a few that Dan's grandson, William May "Willy" Stern included in his book *There's An Old Southern Saying: The Wit and Wisdom of Dan May:*

"What makes old age unbearable is the loss of one's friends. I remember my father saying when he was eighty-four that there were only two people left in Nashville who called him by his first name."

"I just went to see my doctor for a physical examination. Afterwards, the doctor said, 'I don't see anything wrong with you. Why did you come to see me?' I replied, 'I don't feel good.' 'How old are you?' 'Seventy-five' 'Get the hell out of here,' responded the doctor. 'You are never going to feel good.'"

"I've got more friends out here than I do downtown," said Dan in his seventies while at the Jewish cemetery.

When asked in his late seventies how he felt upon waking up in the morning, "surprised" was the response.

"I am going to title my first book *The Joys of Old Age*, and it will consist of nothing but empty pages."

"You can tell when you're getting old because you're either trying to remember someone's name or looking for a place to pee."

"The only way to get thirty minutes' uninterrupted rest in a hospital is to ring for a nurse."

Dan May died in Vanderbilt Hospital following a sudden illness on December 16, 1982. He was eighty-three. Dan was survived by his wife; his son; a daughter, Mrs. Elizabeth May Stern of Westchester, New York; and seven grandchildren. At Dan May's funeral at The Temple on December 20, there was a standing-room-only crowd which included many of Nashville's leading citizens. An old African-American man, wearing a frayed coat and tie, was also there. He told Willy Stern, Dan's grandson, that he worked for May Hosiery Mill for forty years, that Mr. May had always treated him with dignity and respect, and that he was the finest man he'd ever known.

The *Banner* editorial on December 18, titled "Dan May Gave Much to Nashville," spoke of the breadth of his many contributions to his beloved city. It suggested that his greatest may have been "the fulfillment of his dream for a consolidated form of government for Nashville and Davidson County, a concept he envisioned while a member of the county court and a concept he helped translate into reality."

Dan's death notice in the *Banner* identified public education as Dan's primary concern as a politician and said he fought vigorously to fund it adequately. "I can take figures and prove to any businessman that tax money spent for education will bring a faster return than any other public investment," May was quoted as having said.

On February 14, 1983, the Senate of the State of Tennessee unanimously passed Senate Joint Resolution Number Fifteen, written by Senator Douglas Henry Jr. in memory of Dan May, Nashville-Davidson County business and civic leader. Early in 1983, Mrs. May established, as a tribute to her husband, the first lectureship in cardiology at Vanderbilt and summer scholarships in cardiology to give medical students better training and more exposure to academic medicine. Later, the family funded the Dan May Chair of Medicine in the Department of Clinical Pharmacology.

Finally, Herbert Gabhart, chancellor of Belmont University, reflected on his longtime friend in his newspaper column on May 4, 1984. Gabhart wrote, "I was privileged to know this man and call him a 'real cha-rack-ter' as country folks would say, and I mean that description as complimentary in every way. But he was different, unique, humorous, very intelligent, highly successful, community minded, strikingly clever, compassionate, generous, verbally unpredictable, and far-sighted."

Chapter 9

Harvey Pride Jr.
1928–1983

M y wife Irene and I would occasionally attend the Hunt Ball at the Belle Meade Country Club on Iroquois Steeplechase weekends. Harvey Pride Jr. was always there, dressed in his scarlet hunting coat and wearing polished boots. My recollection is that he was constantly talking, and usually had a cigarette in his hand. As usual, he was having the time of his life.

Harvey Pride Jr., the first of two sons of Harvey and Eran Dantzler Pride, was born October 3, 1928. His father was a manufacturer's representative in Nashville. His maternal grandfather, Louis Dantzler, who lived in Moss Point, Mississippi and later New Orleans, was the CEO of Dantzler Lumber Company.[1] Later, his grandsons, Harvey Pride Jr. and Lewis Pride, would inherit equal interests in the company that was sold to International Paper Company.

Harvey and Lewis, who was born February 22, 1933, grew up at their parents' home at 415 Westview Avenue. The house, designed by Donald Southgate, was three doors south of Lynnwood Boulevard. When Harvey was young, he had a horse that his parents kept in a barn behind the house. Childhood friends Dan Denny, Jack Bass, and Neil Cargile Jr. also had ponies or horses. At elegant parties for her children, Mrs. Pride took delight in having a magician named Sander or some other popular local entertainer perform.

Harvey entered the first grade at Parmer School in 1934. In the eighth grade, he played tackle on the Parmer football team. In those years, Parmer played its home games at the "Onion Bowl" on Harding place where the Belle Meade Country Club indoor tennis center is today. His teammates were Jack Bass, Walker Casey, George Cole, Bob Coleman, Neil Craig, Fritz Ingram, Eddie Leverette, Tom McEwen, Warner McNeilly, Julian Scruggs, and Rundle Smith. Harvey's not-so-little brother Lewis was team mascot. Cole and McEwen went on to start on the MBA football team, but not Harvey. He was through with football.

From Parmer, Harvey went to Battle Ground Academy. Having learned to dance at Fortnightly, he became very proficient despite his considerable girth. As a teenager, he loved dancing and did so energetically at dances given by fraternities and sororities, often at the Belle Meade Country Club. Given his size and exuberance, other couples knew to give him a wide berth. Harvey graduated from BGA in 1946, and matriculated at Vanderbilt University before transferring to the University of the South. He later graduated from Tennessee Tech.

After college, Harvey lived with his parents and his brother. Following Mr. Pride's death in 1955, Mrs. Pride and her two sons continued to live on Westview. On one occasion, during those years, Harvey and his young adult friends were playing hide-and-go-seek. Lewis came home, unaware of what was going on, and went to his room. When he opened the door to his closet, there was Harvey's good friend Trilby Williams standing on his shoes. Lewis shouted, "Trilby, get off my shoes. I'm going to have Harvey committed and you're going with him."[2] Lewis tried to keep his distance from Harvey, but that was hard. Once when he came home to find Harvey and his friends having a wild party, Lewis said, "You are all a bunch of juvenile delinquents. Go home."[3] After hearing one too many complaints from Lewis, Harvey and his friends put Saran Wrap under the toilet seat in Lewis' bathroom and short-sheeted his bed.[4] On another occasion, when Mrs. Pride was alive, Harvey and his friends turned out the lights to play hide-and-go-seek, thinking she was asleep. Instead, Mrs. Pride was watching television in the study and had difficulty getting to the bedroom in the dark.[5]

1941 Parmer School football team. Harvey Pride Jr. is the second lineman from the left. Lewis Pride is lying on the grass. Photo courtesy of Phyllis (Mrs. Julian) Scruggs.

In his twenties and thirties, Harvey and Lillias Burns were good friends who attended many parties together. Once, when Harvey had too much to drink, he proposed to Lillias. She loved Harvey but had no intention of marrying him. The next morning, when his head was clear, Harvey sheepishly called her, not exactly sure what he had said the night before. She reminded him.[6] The truth is that Harvey was never known to have a romantic interest with either women or men. He did, however, go to parties with Mannie Jackson and later, with Frances Brooks Corzine after her divorce.[7]

Harvey worked for First American National Bank as a teller in their Belle Meade office, where he personally knew almost all the bank's customers. Harvey had no aspirations for management and was content to service the banking needs of his many friends in the

Belle Meade area. Even at the bank, he usually had a cigarette dangling from his mouth. Occasionally, a friend would call to say that she might be overdrawn. Harvey would check her account and then tell her, "It's OK, but don't go on any binge." Harvey retired from First American in 1964 when he was only thirty-six, thanks to the sale of the Dantzler Lumber Company. Harvey was very proud of his Dantzler ancestry. When asked if his family came from Mississippi, Harvey would say, "My family *is* Mississippi!"[8] Harvey was also a proud Nashvillian. Once, when introduced to a young lady from out of town, Harvey said, "I'll have to accept you even if you are not from Nashville."

Harvey had a wonderful appreciation for fine art and architecture, was smart, and sensitive to the feelings of others despite what he said to the lady who had moved to Nashville. When he liked something or wanted attention, he had a habit of crooking his finger. Harvey loved to gossip and hear gossip but he never did so in a malicious way.

Some of Harvey's devoted friends were Ann and Bob Coleman, Frances Corzine, Betty Ann and Walter Keith, Eleanor and Everett Kelley, Jean and Billy Knox, Eugenia and Ben Moore, Phillys and Julian Scruggs Jr., Trilby and Elliott "Yot" Williams Jr., and Pat and Ronald Voss. For some years Harvey would regularly drop by the Moore's house late in the afternoon for cocktails and, often, stay for dinner.[9]

<hr />

During the late 1950s, when his friends' children were young, Harvey would have elaborate and expensive Christmas parties for them. Eleanor and Everett Kelley's daughters, Craig and Josephine, recalled going to Harvey's parties when they were young. Craig remembered in 2009 that Harvey would buy presents appropriate for each child and that he usually served sugar cookies and ice cream in paper cups for dessert. The mothers would have tenderloin. Bill Jay, a local TV entertainer, would bring puppets to entertain the children who might number fifty or more. If they spilled food or drinks on his exquisite rugs, Harvey never seemed to mind.[10]

Trilby and Elliott Williams Jr. and their son, Elliott Williams III, were invited for Christmas dinner at Harvey's house several times. On such occasions, little Elliott, who was three or four, would sit on several books so he could more easily eat his dinner. He sat there silently except to say, "Yes, sir" or, "No, sir" and watched Uncle Harvey, whom he adored, like a hawk. Julian Scruggs was Elliott's other godfather. Once Harvey told Yot, "Your son has a good godfather (meaning Julian Scruggs). Little Elliott can look at him and learn everything to do right, and look at me, and know everything to do wrong." Little Elliott felt otherwise. Once, he told his parents, "I want to live just like Uncle Harvey. I don't want to ever get married and ever have children."[11] The little children, like Craig and Josephine Kelley, and Elliott Williams III, had their own tables with Christmas favors. For dessert, Harvey served the adults plum pudding with a wonderful whiskey sauce that was ten parts whiskey and one part sugar. In the 1970s, when his own nephews, Dan and Gene Pride, were young, Harvey would give them some plum pudding on Christmas Eve, as he knew that the whiskey would calm their excitement and make them sleep.[12]

Once at a family dinner at Harvey's house, a servant was drunk. Unfortunately, the man's job was to serve food at the dining room table. While serving peas in a silver bowl, he spilled almost as many as he served. Lewis had had enough. He jumped up and told the man to get his things and leave immediately. Harvey took exception at Lewis intervening so blatantly in his home. He yelled, "Lewis, you have no right to fire anyone in my employ." Regardless of which brother prevailed that evening, Harvey definitely had a soft spot for his servants, particularly an aged African-American houseman who had worked for his parents and whom Harvey kept employed, even though the old gentleman was in bad shape physically.

Harvey, who loved to entertain all his life, often held black tie dinner parties on Westview. After his mother's death on March 1, 1961, he renovated the house into a showplace with a particularly handsome walnut-paneled library. The renovated house beautifully showcased Harvey's wonderful art collection and handsome rugs.

While the renovation was underway, Harvey moved next door. When it was time to move back in, his servants were seen carefully carrying one exquisite item at a time across the side yard to the house. Harvey had a big party to celebrate the completion of the renovation. He told friends at the party that he still had to remove an ugly, brownish-gray chandelier in either the dining room or library. Later, when a workman came to take the chandelier down, the man asked Harvey if he was sure he wanted to do this. Harvey said, "Gawd, yes. It's ugly!" The man countered, "Do you realize this is sterling silver?" Harvey, who had not realized that the chandelier was sterling silver, instantly changed his mind. "Don't take it down," he said.[13] Lewis Pride, a savvy attorney, far more practical than Harvey, knew his brother was living beyond his means but was unable to restrain Harvey's spendthrift habits.

Sometime in the 1960s, Harvey invited Ben and Eugenia Moore to take a trip with him in his Lincoln Continental to visit several of the antebellum plantations along the James River, including Shirley Plantation, and to see Williamsburg and Richmond. One day in Tidewater, Virginia, Harvey served watercress and tomato sandwiches and stuffed eggs with caviar, washed down with champagne, for a picnic lunch. They were guests for dinner at Shirley Plantation, where they ate off the same china plates that were used when Robert E. Lee was a guest. They also were guests of Harrison Tyler, a grandson of U.S. President John Tyler. At Williamsburg, they had dinner at the Commonwealth Club, and went to a showroom featuring fine antiques from London's Stair & Company. There, Harvey bought a breakfront that Eugenia remembers to have cost $250,000. When she later questioned him about having paid so much, Harvey said, "Eugenia, you just don't understand its provenance." At Bruton Parish Church in restored Williamsburg, they attended a Sunday morning service where U.S. President Lyndon Johnson was present. Eugenia remembers that the minister, in his sermon, told President Johnson to "get out of Vietnam."

On New Year's Eve at Harvey's house, his friends would shoot bottle rockets, sometimes at the guests of Florence and Roland Lamb next door or, if the Lambs were inside, at the house itself. On one occasion, when Roland felt he had been bombarded enough, he appeared at the door waving a white towel. Another time, when Roland and

Florence were having a dinner party, Harvey's friends moved his Lincoln Continental to the Lamb driveway and hid the keys. The next day, Harvey sent flowers to the Lambs for the inconvenience his friends caused when the Lambs' dinner guests had difficulty getting around Harvey's automobile to go home.[14] In truth, Harvey often felt obligated to send flowers to the Lambs following his parties.

At a Fourth of July party Harvey hosted, two of his friends threw firecrackers into the steam furnace in the basement. There was an explosion and, to Harvey's horror, steam began to come out of the radiators on the first floor.[15] At another Fourth of July party on Westview, someone put three lit bottle rockets in a cake container that had been left on the floor of Harvey's entrance hall. Well, the container hit the ceiling and came back down just as fast, leaving a big black mark where it hit the floor.

Harvey's fiftieth birthday in 1978 was special. Ten friends gave him a party at Phillys and Julian Scruggs' home. Everyone had a great time, particularly when Trilby Williams jumped out of a cardboard box wrapped in tissue paper to resemble a big birthday cake. She wore a tight black lace dress, black mesh stockings and high heels. Needless to say, she did not strip. The birthday napkins read, "Oh, my Gawd, I'm 50." As party favors, each couple was given a green pennant of the 1941 Parmer School football team. Someone had bumper stickers made that read, "Harvey Pride is 50," and put them on each car at the party. One couple did not discover their sticker until they registered at a hotel 450 miles from Nashville.[16] On another occasion, one of Harvey's friends stole a "Harvey's will never know completion" sign from the department store and installed it in Harvey's front yard. He was thrilled.[17]

There was a blacktie wedding party at Harvey's home that Trilby and Yot Williams had not been invited to. Trilby, being miffed at not being on the guest list, decided to have some fun at Harvey's expense. She concocted a plan that her younger brother, Bill Elliston and his friend, Louis B. Todd, carried out.

Trilby secured a crate of half-grown chickens from somewhere. The boys, then MBA students, took them to Harvey's house, slipped in the back door, and turned them loose in the front hall. One friend sitting on the front hall steps immediately saw the chickens and commented, "I know I've had a drink or two but I see live chickens in here." Harvey saw the chickens and exclaimed in his high-pitched voice, "My Gawd, there are chickens in my front hall." As Bill and Louis ran back to the car, Bill looked in the dining room window and saw a chicken hopping across the dining room table.

The next morning, Trilby found the chickens in her house. When she called Harvey for an explanation, he said, "Trilby, don't you say a word, I know it was either you or Walter Keith who played that trick on me."[18] The chicken episode became the talk of Belle Meade, and Harvey relished the attention. Considerably later, when he discovered that Bill and Louis were the actual culprits, he sent them each a bottle of champaign with a note thanking them for enlivening the party.

Often at his dinner parties, Harvey served a different wine with each course and had beautiful centerpieces and flowers on the table. On one such occasion, one of his friends, having had too much alcohol, began throwing rolls over the large centerpiece. Harvey said, "You are all peasants. I'm never going to have you again." Of course, he did. On other formal occasions at Harvey's house, he was known to walk around carrying a lit candelabra that he used to light his cigarettes.[19] Occasionally, Harvey and his close friends played strip poker at his house. One evening, Trilby walked in and found Harvey sitting at the table with three friends wearing only a pair of pants. He wailed, "They have won nearly all my clothes!"

Harvey's generosity to his friends and their children was matched by his interest in Christ Episcopal Church; Cheekwood, where he served on the board; the Nashville Humane Association, where he was president; the Bill Wilkerson Hearing and Speech Center; and Historic Belmont. Once on leaving a funeral service at Christ Church, Harvey overheard a lady complain that the service was over almost before she got comfortably seated. Defensive about his beloved church, Harvey could not resist telling her, "We Episcopalians believe that if you knew a person well enough when he was alive, you don't need to learn about his life at his funeral."

⸺◦◦◦⸺

One of the loves of Harvey's life was his membership in the Hillsboro Hounds. He was a regular on his horse during their hunts at Lynnville, and would arrive with a trunk full of feed for his horse in that big Lincoln. Harvey's horse friends said that the trunk of his car was always a wreck.

Harvey Pride Jr. jumping a fence with the Hillsboro Hounds. Photo courtesy of Amy Scruggs McKelvey.

On one occasion, while driving back from either Lynnville or Cornersville to Nashville, Harvey temporarily lost control of his car and went into a ditch. When Trilby saw his car sometime later, she noticed that the car's tailpipe was full of dirt and grass. Harvey told her, "Just don't ask me about it. It's not important." A worse mishap occurred on another return trip from fox hunting. That evening, Harvey was arrested for drunk driving, and put in the Williamson County jail because he didn't have the money to pay his bail. Instead, he called Lewis and asked him to come pay his fine and get him out. Lewis said it wasn't convenient to drive down to Franklin and that he would come in the morning. Harvey ranted and raved to no avail. Two of Harvey's friends heard about his incarceration, and thought-fully had delivered to him a cornbread cake with a file inside. The jailor, who delivered the cake to Harvey, asked if he might have a piece. Harvey said, "Gawd, yes." When the jailor cut a slice, he heard a clink. He was not amused. Harvey spent the night in jail and was extremely miffed when Lewis showed up the next morning.[20]

The *Nashville Banner* wrote of Harvey's love for fox (or coyote) hunting after his death. The article said that Pride "scorned a physical shell less than ideal for horsemanship to master the sport of following hounds across the demanding Middle Tennessee terrain. In spite of his portly build, Pride, with skill and grace, rode mounts ranging in difficulty from his gentle and beloved mare Eran[21] to the rip-snorting Major Grey, a handful for all who tried him." In his horseback riding days, the article continued, "Pride was often the first at scenes of action, and at least once was awarded the fox brush, a hunt trophy he proudly tied to his car's antenna."[22] The fox brush was actually the tail of a fox. The day he was awarded the prize, he took the brush home and put it in the freezer unit of his refrigerator. The next morning, Harvey's maid happened to open the freezer door. Seeing what she thought was the tail of a puppy, she naturally screamed. Harvey thoughtfully gave her the day off.

Nashville artist Sandor Bodo found Harvey's distinctive figure irresistible, and included him in the background of many fox hunting scenes. The last few years of his life, health problems forced Harvey to give up riding. He would still participate, following the hunters in his Lincoln Continental. Earlier, Harvey had been able to easily clear hurdles on Major Grey.

In about 1968, the Roland Lambs sold their home next door to Harvey to Dr. Charles E. and Ann Wells, who were then the parents of two little boys, Wyatt and Harwell, then ages four and three. At the time of their purchase of the home, Ann was pregnant with her daughter, Ann. Three years later, Mrs. Wells was Swan Ball co-chairman. She and Gertrude Caldwell, chairman of the Swan Ball that year, asked Harvey to host the Patron's Party. Because he cared about Cheekwood, loved hosting parties, and liked Ann and Gertrude, Harvey accepted.[23] He decided to invite his core group of friends even though they were not patrons. He told them it was safer to invite them than to risk what they might do if not invited.[24] Mr. and Mrs. Wentworth Caldwell Sr. were also at that party. Later, Mrs. Caldwell commented, "No one entertains like this anymore." Of course, the flower arrangements that evening were gorgeous. They invariably were at Harvey's parties.

———————

When Harvey's nephew, Dan Pride, was five years old, he got the biggest Christmas surprise of his young life. On Christmas morning, Sissie and Mack Anderton, owners of Brownland Farm, showed up pulling a horse trailer. The next thing Dan knew, there was a pony standing outside with its mane carefully decorated with red and green ribbons. Harvey, who always spent Christmas Eve night with Lewis and his family, explained that the pony was his Christmas gift to Dan.

———————

Lewis Pride died February 8, 1978, two weeks short of his forty-fifth birthday, leaving a widow, Missy Holeman Pride, and their two small sons, Dan and Gene. Several years later, Harvey decided, as a treat, to take his nephews in his new automobile to New Orleans. The plan was for Dan and Gene to stay there a couple of nights and then fly home and for Harvey, after shopping on Royal Street to his heart's content, to drive home at his leisure. The trip didn't start well. An hour or so out of Nashville, Harvey remembered that he had left the boys' airline tickets at home. They turned around and came back for the tickets. The Prides finally got to Pass Christian, Mississippi, where Harvey showed his nephews the Dantzler family graveyard and the old Dantzler Lumber Company headquarters, and introduced them to Harvey's aunt Martha (Mrs. A. M.) Dantzler. The next day, Harvey, Dan and Gene drove to New Orleans, where they stayed in the Royal Sonesta Hotel on Bourbon Street. The boys' most vivid memory of the trip was having dinner at Commander's Palace. To their astonishment, Uncle Harvey instructed their waiter there to, under no circumstances, bring ketchup to their table. Dan later concluded that Uncle Harvey thought ketchup was too plebeian to be served in such an exclusive restaurant. For several years, Dan and Gene gave Uncle Harvey at Christmas a bottle of ketchup, wrapped as a gift.[25]

Harvey loved to take short trips to New Orleans and New York to shop, eat at the great restaurants, and see plays and performances. Once when he was in New York with his friend Julian Morton of Knoxville, Harvey called room service to order breakfast. Unfortunately, the woman could not understand his Southern accent. Frustrated, Harvey hung up and called Morton to order for him.[26]

With Lewis not around to restrain his luxurious lifestyle, Harvey's finances became tight. To conserve his diminishing capital, he sold the house on Westview and moved to a handsome but slightly smaller house he built in Gloucester Square, Fred Webber's development on Golf Club Lane. This house also had a large and lovely library in the back. Harvey lived there until the house burned. The cause of the fire was unknown. As a result of the fire, Harvey moved to a much more modest apartment in Chowning Square. One evening, when he returned to Chowning Square, Harvey saw fire engines and quickly realized that his apartment was on fire. It was totally destroyed and his dog, Toodles, a beloved Yorkshire terrier, perished. Harvey's final move was to the Blackstone, an old apartment building facing West End in Acklen Park.

Late in his life, some remember Harvey riding an elephant at the Steeplechase grounds during a circus benefit for the Humane Association. He looked terrified. Teenie Hooker Buchtel was astride another elephant that day. What a sight.

Harvey Pride Jr. was discovered dead of a heart attack in his car on a cold December night in 1983 at the age of fifty-five. He was buried in Section Eleven of Mt. Olivet Cemetery in his Hillsboro Hounds scarlet attire, complete with polished hunting boots. An editorial in the *Nashville Banner* on January 3, 1984, said "With his funeral plans as in his life, Pride, an altruist, who worked diligently for a half dozen local charities, showed considerable flair."[27] Trilby probably expressed the sentiments of all of Harvey's close friends when she said, "Harvey was the nicest person I ever knew." He left much of his fine art and silver to Cheekwood, and bequeathed his fine collection of lead soldiers to the Cumberland Museum and Science Center.

Chapter 10

Frederick Tupper Saussy III
1936–2007

No doubt about it; Tupper Saussy's house had to have been the most exciting spot on Belle Meade Boulevard.

Frederick Tupper Saussy III was a native of Statesboro, Georgia, where his family was both prominent and respected. His maternal grandfather was Dr. A. J. Mooney, the town physician. His parents were Mary Melinda "Mary Lind" Mooney and Frederick Tupper Saussy Jr. Tupper III was born July 3, 1936. After growing up in Tampa, Florida, he attended the University of the South at Sewanee, where he had a jazz combo that produced a university-subsidized album. *Jazz at Sewanee* included several compositions he wrote. A cartoonist for the school paper and fraternity member as well, Tupper was very popular.

While at Sewanee, Tupper met George Crook of Nashville. When Tupper moved to Nashville following his graduation in 1958, George introduced him to Lola Haun, who was cute, adventurous and wealthy. She also drove a Corvette that Tupper liked.[1]

In Nashville, Francis Carter, headmaster of Montgomery Bell Academy, hired Tupper to teach English and history. Carter got more than he bargained for. He knew Tupper was bright, but he wasn't prepared for his flamboyance and casual attitude toward teaching. Although Tupper left after one year to go into the advertising business, the students never forgot him or his unconventional ways. Charlie Wray, who was in Tupper's freshman English class, remembered that Tupper sometimes taught Shakespeare while seated in a chair on the top of his desk. Tupper also enjoyed drawing bull's-eyes on the blackboard, which he would then try to hit with chalk thrown from the back of the room. On Mondays, he arrived at the school parking lot in his red MG. The boys occasionally saw a pair of ladies' hose hanging from the rearview mirror. After word of Tupper's eccentricities became well-known on campus, some students picked up his MG and put it in the gym lobby. Senior Sam Pickering Jr., a member of the Glee Club that Tupper organized, took mental notes of Tupper's antics and filed them away for another day.

One day a student's mother came to see Tupper regarding her son's grade, which she felt was unfair. She asked Tupper to change the grade. When he refused to do so, she, according to him, "ranted and raved." He told her, "Madam, control your ire." That set her off even more and, when Tupper last saw her, she was headed to the headmaster's office.[2]

While teaching at MBA, Tupper and his girlfriend Lola were having fun in Nashville. They became engaged over the school year and married on June 26, 1959, in Nashville. Only nineteen, she was the daughter of Julia Fay and Cale Haun, one of the founders of Equitable Securities Corporation. The wedding was huge, remembered Patrick Anderson, one of Tupper's Sewanee fraternity brothers. "There were countless parties that the most famous people in town were giving for them," Anderson said.[3] Anderson described Lola, who was an only child, as very bright but a little spoiled and undisciplined.[4] She grew up in a large home in Belle Meade that later became the chancellor's residence for Vanderbilt University. Two older friends, both Sewanee men, Ed Nelson and John Jay Hooker Jr., were ushers at the wedding.

In 1959, Tupper, who was a little too creative for the strict and conservative prep school, joined McDonald and Associates, a Nashville advertising company, as their creative director. This was a great move for Tupper and the agency. By 1963, he owned half of the company.[5] That same year, Tupper came up with the advertising slogan for Purity Dairies, the cow that was always saying, "Don't pay no attention to kangaroos." Another client was May

Lola and Tupper Saussy. Photo courtesy of Haun Saussy.

Hosiery Mills, where Tupper became friends with CEO Jack May. Tupper successfully balanced his advertising career with his musical career, which he kept alive with recording sessions and playing dates in the evenings.

Flush with quick success and Lola's money, the Saussys moved into the old Dr. Cleo Miller house on Belle Meade Boulevard in the summer of 1960. It quickly became a gathering place for late-night parties, often following the Swan Ball or events at the Belle Meade Country Club. I remember driving by the house late at night and seeing all the lights turned on, and music and noise pouring into the neighborhood. There was always lots of liquor, and Tupper was always the center of attention. Often such celebrities as Dave Brubeck, Arthur Fiedler, or author Kingsley Amis would be there. The Saussys had servants who ran the house.[6] Their houseman later drove "hookups" for their two children, Haun and Melinda Cavanaugh Saussy, whose nickname was "Vana."

Once, during the 1960s, Pat Spickard Wildman and her husband Jim were invited to the Saussys for dinner. Pat was apprehensive about going, as the Saussys were considered a little wild. She and Jim went, however, and everything went fine—other than Tupper unsuccessfully attempting to get Pat to try some marijuana.

David Halberstam, a bright Harvard-educated reporter for *The Nashville Tennessean*, was a more typical guest at Saussy parties. Tupper "came and charmed Nashville," wrote Halberstam. "He played the piano and married a beautiful woman. They were the golden couple. Everything seemed to be his."[7]

Between 1964 and 1970, Tupper produced a number of records: *Discover Tupper Saussy*, *Said I to Shostakovich*, *The Swinger's Guide to Mary Poppins*, *The Moth Confesses* and *The Neon Philharmonic* among them.

In the late 1960s, Tupper was keyboardist for the psychedelic pop band called The Neon Philharmonic, whose vocalist was Don Gant. Saussy's *Morning Girl*, recorded by his group, hit Number Nineteen on the pop charts. *Morning Girl* earned them two Grammy nominations against competition that included The Beatles, Chicago, and Led Zeppelin.[8] Saussy wrote other songs performed by the Nashville Symphony, Chet Atkins, Perry Como, and Ray Stevens. On January 13 and 14, 1969, Tupper played *Hausgeists: Piano Concerto No. 1* at performances of the Nashville Symphony.[9]

"Tupper was a bright star in Nashville. He was busy composing symphony concertos, painting portraits, writing books, and designing nationally recognized advertisements. He appeared to

Frederick Tupper Saussy III in 1965. Photo courtesy of the Nashville Public Library, Special Collections.

have more talent than ten men," a friend said. Tupper was content. "I had all the material success and enjoyment I needed." It was while he lived the good life that Tupper wrote a novella titled *The Gimmes*. It would evolve into a play at Nashville's John Galt West

End Theatre. Tupper recalled in March of 1986, "I sent the novella to a publisher, and he said it's too adult for children and too naïve for an adult book. So, I set it on the back burner for a while."[10] Tupper's sister-in-law, Jeanie Cammack, agreed with the publisher. She thought it was terrible.

Always open to a new and exciting idea, Tupper and Mary Walton Caldwell opened, in 1971, the Ritz Café, a restaurant on Elliston Place where the Gold Rush Restaurant is today. He was said to have considered building a shark-filled moat around the restaurant. Tupper said he "just wanted a place to eat free." Quickly, the Ritz became the restaurant of choice for his wide circle of friends. Mary Walton, a renowned cook, was the chef. The interior of the cafe displayed Tupper's own artwork, "a whimsical series of watercolors of brown paper bags." In 1996, Mary Walton remembered, "The last I heard of those paintings, they were shown at Cheekwood." A friend of Tupper's who frequented the Ritz often said, "The Ritz was so much fun, but Tupper was so careless he never paid any withholding tax on his employees." When the café closed in March 1974, Mary Walton would not talk about why that happened. Instead, she moved to La Jolla, California.[11]

The fast life also had its price on Tupper's relationship with Lola. Their marriage crumbled, ending in divorce in 1972.[12] Sometime later, Tupper wrote a play that he planned to show locally. Frederique "Freddie" Blanco auditioned for a part. She was the daughter of a prominent physician in San Juan, Puerto Rico, and had come to Nashville to visit her aunt, Merida Blanco Oman, wife of prominent Nashville businessman John Oman. Freddie decided to stay and got a teaching job at Harpeth Hall. A friend described her as "quite striking, not unlike Bianca Jagger." She and Tupper fell in love and married. After the marriage, Ann Street remembered the watercolor of Lola and Tupper sitting at a French café that was hanging on a wall at the Ritz Café. She went down there and repainted Lola's face to resemble Freddie.[13]

Ann Street, Nashville's finest portrait painter and wife of architect Bob Street, was responsible for interesting Tupper in the theater.

A member of the amateur theater group, Circle Players, which was putting on *Cactus Flower*, Ann learned that the leading man had become ill with pneumonia. Because the group was desperate to find a replacement, Ann said, "I'll get Tupper. He can do anything." Ann first called Lola who said, "He won't do it." To Ann's surprise and pleasure, Tupper did agree to play the part. He became fascinated with the theater and began writing plays. At one time, he told Nashville artist Paul Harmon that "Egyptomania" was going to sweep the nation and he was going to write a play about Egypt. Then, while sitting next to the artist on a flight to New York, Tupper told Paul that he thought pirates were going to be big so he was going to write a play about pirates.[14] He didn't do that but, in 1972, he did publish a play, *To Watch a Beautiful Sunrise*, through Samuel French Inc. This was a comedy revolving around a radical anarchist with the House of the Rising Sons who agrees to kill his own step-father. The darkness of the play spoke to Tupper's own mood.

———————

By 1974, Tupper was clearly upset and agitated about the IRS. One day, George Crook asked him to write some copy for one of his advertising firm's clients. George remembered, "Tupper started talking about this book he was going to write. He had almost memorized the Constitution and thought the IRS was illegal. He was almost rabid on the subject."[15]

The same year, Congress passed the Privacy Act of 1974, which Tupper pounced on. He concluded that it "required the IRS to notify citizens that information provided on tax forms might be given to other government agencies, corporations or foreign governments." This did not suit him at all as it was, in his opinion, a flagrant violation of his personal freedom.

By the fall of 1974, having long ago dropped out of advertising and having shut down the Ritz Café, Tupper cast his eyes on Sewanee Mountain. In November, he bought an abandoned Cumberland Presbyterian Church in Cowan, Tennessee, six miles down the mountain from Sewanee. The building had a seating capacity of seventy-five and thirteen antique stained-glass windows. Tupper, having become fascinated with the building, did a little remodeling and renamed it Appletree Theater. He would be founder and managing director. He hired John Nee as his chef. Because he and Freddie were still living in Nashville, he also needed a resident director. Agnes Wilcox would fill that role.[16] Appletree got off to a promising start. In February, his production of the comedy *Butterflies Are Free* was held over through Sunday, February 26. Saussy was pleased, saying, "The added two weeks will accommodate ticket buyers who are coming to the show in record numbers in spite of terrible weather."

In December, he held his first one-man show at Cheekwood Museum of Art. "I love containers and a house is a container, a package," said Tupper, a multi-faceted artist, songwriter, composer, and former advertising executive who had studied with Walter Sunderland and Alain DeLeiris. Tupper was so talented as an artist that some of his works are in the permanent collection at the Tennessee State Museum.

Tupper continued to paint in 1975. In September, the *Nashville Banner* featured a picture of his watercolor titled "Mobile Home."[17] A day earlier, the *Banner* showcased a picture of a watercolor of a brown paper bag, one of Tupper's works in watercolor and acrylics that would be exhibited at the University Club beginning on Sunday, September 14, continuing through October.

<hr/>

With so many things swirling around in his head, Tupper had difficulty focusing on painting. "All Tupper wanted to talk about was taxes and the monetary system."[18] This was a bad omen. Pulled by the idea of writing satires of the IRS, Tupper decided he could do so with fewer distractions in Sewanee than he could in Nashville. He and Freddie moved there in 1976, renting what he described as "a lovely little house in downtown Sewanee, if there is such a thing as downtown in Sewanee." He also leased a building across from the post office, where he published a weekly newspaper in which he could express his views on tax issues. He produced *The Gimmes* at the Appletree; it was a brutal satire on the U.S. Government, and on opening night, two IRS agents were said to have attended.[19]

By the time he had moved to the mountain, Tupper had developed the habit of never paying bills with his own personal checks. Instead, he always paid in cash, with a money order, or by giving creditors a stack of small second-party checks he had endorsed. Bill Barnes, a Nashville graphic designer who did some work for Tupper, was one of those who was always paid this way. The FBI later called on Barnes to ask about his dealings with Mr. Saussy.[20]

In his antagonism toward the government, Tupper also got the misguided idea of having his own personalized license plate. He got rid of his Tennessee license plate or, at least, took it off his car. One day, while driving down the mountain, a Tennessee highway patrolman pulled Tupper over for having an invalid license plate that read "Kingdom of God." Tupper argued that he was beholden to God and not to the State of Tennessee. Despite Tupper's charm, the highway patrolman gave him a ticket.[21]

In 1978, Saussy filed suit against the Tennessee Department of Revenue. Tupper contended that the state illegally seized money from his bank account for back sales tax payments. The suit claimed that Mr. Saussy's civil rights were violated when the state seized his bank account funds because he was not granted a hearing. Saussy further argued that the state couldn't force him to be taxed on Federal Reserve notes, but only on gold or silver."

On December 4, U.S. District Judge Charles Neese granted Saussy a hearing in his suit against the State Department of Revenue. The hearing was held on Wednesday, December 6. In his recommendation, U.S. Magistrate Robert P. Murrian said Saussy's claim was invalid because Congress had the power "to coin money and regulate the value thereof." Saussy was "elated at the chance to have a hearing." He felt this "would be a rare chance for a court to decide in favor of the U.S. Constitution and put an end to inflation and recession and make our currency redeemable in lawful money." Saussy, who represented himself in the suit, also asked for a jury trial.[22] Needless to say, Tupper's lawsuit was unsuccessful.

IRS agents began coming by Tupper's home soon after he and Freddie moved to Sewanee. In the later 1970s, the visits became more frequent. Freddie remembered, "They would wait until they knew my husband was not there and then come and harass me and my children. Once they told me I might as well leave because they were going to take our home anyway. I held out my husband's guitar and said, 'Take this, and leave us alone!' They took the guitar and we haven't seen it since." She said agents would show up at odd times under peculiar circumstances. One Saturday afternoon, she was serving lunch on the front porch to a group of Tupper's friends from Nashville. "I noticed two men I didn't recognize, but I thought 'Well, Tupper's brought two more in,' and served them too. One of them said, 'Are you going to feed me?' Someone said they were IRS agents. I jerked the plate away from him! The other one was eating a piece of corn on the cob, and he said, 'Oh, please let me keep my corn.'"[23]

<hr/>

To give him additional seconds to escape through the back door of his office in Sewanee should the IRS arrive, Tupper had an extra front door built as an entrance to a small foyer.

When Tupper was not at his office or home, he was usually at the Appletree Theater. In 1979, he wrote a musical revue *Precious Moments* that ran so successfully at the Appletree that it was held over for two days.[24] In September, Tupper brought his two-person version of *Precious Moments* to Cheekwood. in Nashville. The *Nashville Banner* reported, "It is a star-studded revue of crucial events between men and women."[25]

Tupper Saussy wrote a book based on his constitutional studies. Published in 1980, *The Miracle on Main Street* sold, according to Saussy, more than 107,000 copies at seven dollars a copy and, in Tupper's thinking, became a handbook for the nationwide monetary and anti-tax movements.[26] Tupper also launched a magazine, *The Main Street Journal,* which espoused the same theory. Saussy's book was an argument for restoring the gold and silver monetary standard laid down in Article One, Section Ten of the U.S. Constitution that says: "No state shall make anything but gold or silver coin a tender in payment of debts." With publication of his book, Tupper gained national visibility. Tupper was sure that the book heightened the interest of the IRS. He said, "I'm told I've been selected by the IRS for Project ACE. It targets certain people who have given the appearance of aiding or abetting or being in sympathy with the so-called tax protest movement. These people are singled out and all the stops are pulled out to get them in court in any fashion they can." Wilson Fadely, public affairs officer at the IRS Headquarters in Washington, D.C., flatly denied Saussy's charge. He said, "I have never heard of Project ACE, and we have no illegal tax-protester program. We do give a lot of emphasis on getting a case against the leaders of tax revolt. They use frivolous arguments like gold and silver in a lot of cases." Saussy insisted he was not leading a tax revolt. "I am not a tax protestor. I don't think income taxes are illegal. It's the Privacy Act, and giving information to the IRS that I'm afraid of."[27]

Tupper would still come to Nashville from time to time to see friends. In September 1981, he displayed a paper-bag poster for the "Sack Lunch and Symposium Series" sponsored by the Nashville Symphony Guild. He said, "Copies are ten dollars each."[28]

In the summer of 1984, Saussy's relations with the IRS took a far more serious turn. On July 31 that year, the IRS contacted Saussy and challenged him on his tax returns. It was exactly then that what Saussy termed a "religious war" erupted. Federal prosecutors called it "tax evasion." The IRS charged Saussy for failing to file tax returns for 1977 through 1979. The IRS jailed him and threatened him for willfully failing to pay his federal taxes.[29]

Word of Tupper's arrest quickly reached his friends in Nashville, who could not understand why in the world he preferred to risk imprisonment for failing to file his federal income tax returns rather than bite his tongue and pay them.

With his trial scheduled to start in November, Saussy quickly ran into trouble with U.S. District Judge Thomas Hull of Greeneville, who presided over the Winchester, Tennessee, courtroom. The trial was rescheduled, and in January 1985, Hull ruled that Huntsville's Lowell Becraft could not represent Saussy because he had a court date conflict. Robert Peters of Winchester was appointed in his stead. Saussy, however, wanted Peters to be a major defense witness, since he had discussed his case with the Winchester attorney many times. Saussy and Peters agreed that since a lawyer cannot testify for his client, Peters could not represent him. At the time the Winchester court convened, Saussy was still without legal representation. He requested another continuance, which Hull refused. Despite Saussy's protests that he was without counsel, Hull ordered that the trial proceed. Saussy, who was frightened, turned to his family and said, "I can't get a fair trial here. I'm leaving."[30] At that point, Hull instructed FBI agents and U.S. Marshals to detain him. Saussy took three steps away from the defense table and he was arrested. FBI agents and U.S. Marshals attempted to separate Tupper from his family. Frederique said her children, Pierre-Phillipe, 10, and Laurent, 6, were injured in the scuffle and she required medical attention at Emerald-Hodgson Hospital in Sewanee after being hit in the abdomen.

Meanwhile, seventy Saussy admirers in the court room created bedlam with shouts of "The Gestapo has taken over" and "The judge is a communist." Afraid of what might happen, the Franklin County Sheriff's Office called for help from six neighboring towns before attempting to move Saussy to Chattanooga. Hull declared Saussy in contempt of court and ordered him to serve ninety days.[31] After the disturbance died down, Saussy was driven to Hamilton County Jail in Chattanooga. There, he complained that he was denied his request, made on religious and health grounds, for a dozen oranges, grapefruit, and banana daily. Possibly for security reasons, Saussy was transferred to the federal penitentiary in Atlanta.

On March 10, 1985, an indictment repeating the charges against Saussy was handed down by a federal grand jury in Chattanooga. In the indictment, Saussy was charged with willfully failing to file income tax returns for 1977, 1978, and 1979.

After serving forty-eight days of his ninety-day contempt of court sentence, Saussy was released in mid-March when supporters posted his $20,000 bail.[32] Still defiant, he said he was ready to go back to jail if that was what it would take to continue his fight against the IRS.

For the next twenty-one months, there was seemingly endless turmoil with charges and counter-charges. Saussy was representing himself along with co-counsel William Waller of Denver; Judge Hull advised Saussy to "hire a good lawyer and listen to him." Saussy said that friends were trying to contact Boston attorney Alan

Dershowitz, but that he "couldn't afford Dershowitz" even if he had been available. In truth, Waller had "consulting privileges" with Dershowitz.[33]

On May 2, 1985, dissidents from thirty-two states convened on Chattanooga in automobiles, vans and campers to attend a two-day Political Justice Symposium in support of Saussy.[34] Described as primarily middle-class folks, they tended to be libertarians, members of the Populist and Republican parties, or independents. Most had grievances with the IRS and the U.S. courts that they were only too happy to recount. Some demanded the abolishment of income taxes and of the Federal Reserve System, and a return to the gold and silver standard. Others were opponents of gun control and abortion. Still others were proponents of home schools. Many wanted an end to "Nazi-like" government. A good many had prison records or had been charged with tax-related offenses.[35] It definitely was not your normal Mountain City Club crowd.

The symposium was deliberately timed to take place before Saussy faced trial on May 29. He spoke at the symposium, as did former U.S. Congressman George Hansen of Idaho; a retired FBI agent; and a flamboyant anti-IRS preacher from Georgia. Saussy asked the crowd for contributions to help him pay for his legal expenses. His co-counsel William Waller had agreed to take the case on a promise of payment from supporters' contributions. Saussy said, "The fight we are waging is a holy war, not unlike the struggle of Soviet dissidents." He also said, "I'm not asking you for a loan. I'm asking for a commitment." Saussy argued that the federal courts had no jurisdiction because no accuser had been named. He also claimed he was given illegal notice of the charges, claiming that indictments must be hand-delivered, not mailed. "All I want is a fair trial. All this group wants is for this country to return to righteous law as it was given to us in the Constitution." At a banquet on Saturday night, Frederique Saussy held everyone's attention when she said that she had trained her older son, Pierre-Phillipe, how to recognize license tag numbers of IRS agents who continually harassed her while Tupper was away. The crowd roared its delight when the boys took the microphone and expressed their appreciation to their dad's supporters.[36]

Prosecutors claimed in the first day of Saussy's trial in U.S. District Court that he knew he was breaking the law when he filed federal income tax forms that did not reveal his income. "He knew how to file returns correctly," said Assistant U.S. Attorney John Littleton. According to the government, Saussy had income of $21,404, $51,063 and $37,558 for 1977, 1978 and 1979, the years he did not file taxes. Littleton noted that Saussy had filed returns from 1972 through 1976. The defense was scheduled to present its case on May 30. If convicted, Saussy could be sent to prison for one year and fined $10,000 for each misdemeanor count. In his opening statement, William Waller argued that Saussy was simply protecting himself from self-incrimination when he filed income tax returns that did not show his income. Instead, Saussy, Waller said, attached documents claiming he could not pay under terms of the U.S. Constitution, contending that the Constitution makes it illegal to use anything except gold and silver to pay debts. Waller told the full courtroom, "The question is whether a man can be put in jail for doing what he honestly believes is his constitutional right." Tupper also argued that tax returns were given to other governmental agencies, and to state and foreign governments. He "believed he had a Fifth Amendment right to demand that the government assure him the information on the return would be used only to compute taxes." Waller called the government's charge that Saussy was a tax protester an "invidious classification."[37]

Saussy's demand that the government write him to assure that the information on his tax return not be used for any other purpose than to compute taxes came from the Privacy Act of 1974. "You have to understand the Privacy Act of 1974," Saussy said. "That act required the IRS to notify citizens that information provided on tax forms might be given to other government agencies, corporations or foreign governments."[38]

The result was that Saussy was convicted for failure to pay federal income taxes on an income of $21,404 for 1977. He was acquitted on charges of failure to pay taxes for 1978 and 1979 as jurors found Saussy broke no law because he filed the forms. After his appeal failed, he was ordered in 1987 to begin serving a one-year sentence in federal prison in Atlanta.

Judge Hull ordered Saussy to surrender himself to the U.S. Marshal in Chattanooga or to the Federal Prison Camp Building in Atlanta on April 10, 1987, to begin a one-year prison sentence. He was fined $10,000. Saussy was also ordered to pay $6,360 in court expenses. Judge Hull did, however, give defense attorney William Waller twenty days to file motions for reduction or elimination of trial costs. Assistant U.S. Attorney John Littleton said of Saussy, "You can forget rehabilitation. He has been uncooperative with the probation department. He has been unrepentant. He has taken the position of messiah of a movement and in so doing has corrupted others and misled them." Hull told Saussy, "You are almost victim of your own intelligence."[39]

Hull allowed Saussy to remain free on a $20,000 corporate bond posted before his trial. Saussy appealed to the U.S. Circuit Court of Appeals, which upheld the conviction.

Feeling he was unjustly convicted, Tupper came to the conclusion that prison would not be the right place for him to push his brand of civil activism and his view of morality. Instead, he needed, he decided, "a term in the desert, like the Apostle Paul."[40]

So, the first week in April, Saussy went to the Atlanta prison early one morning and videotaped himself outside the gates. "I surrendered myself openly and notoriously to the institution," Tupper wrote afterward in a letter to several Tennessee newspapers, federal prosecutors, and U.S. District Judge Thomas Hull. He then dropped out of sight. He did, however, write several other letters labeled "Statements From a Banished Citizen." In them, he expressed his interpretation of the laws he was accused of breaking.[41] Saussy's attorney, William Waller, said, "I just assumed something had happened to him or he'd moved out of the country and we'd never hear from him again." Waller called Saussy "one of the most brilliant men I've ever been around."[42]

On April 15, 1987, Chattanooga television station WRCB aired a homemade videotape that came in the mail with a note from Saussy. Nashville's WTVF also aired the tape, which showed Saussy outside the federal prison camp, knocking on the door and asking to be let in. Standing beside a sign on the door, he turned to the camera and said, "Look, I'm here and they are not. I'm leaving." The note also said, "The U.S. Attorney's charges against me were feloniously false, fraudulent and obstructed justice. I am going into seclusion to finish my own book about more than three years of federal atrocities against the innocent Saussy family."[43]

Saussy claimed he was "following divine law" and listening to "a higher calling," that caused him to rebel against the "human law" instituted by the federal government. In response to their tyranny, Saussy used *The Gimmes* to reflect what he called the "downswing" in every man's life. "There is a lot of anger in that play. There's a lot of impatience with people who have no self esteem," Saussy told Mark Zabriskie in March 1986.[44]

The play was a hard attack on the establishment, in turn lambasting politicians, judges, lawyers, entrepreneurs and materialistic women. The play was also cynical. Saussy said, "A lot of people go to see it as a comedy. I take it very seriously. I only laugh five or six times during a performance."[45]

Later in April, William R. "Bill" Saussy, Tupper's brother, received a phone call from Tupper asking him to come to the Atlanta's Hartsfield International Airport with boxes of a book Tupper had either written or edited, a biography of James Earl Ray entitled *Tennessee Waltz: The Making of a Political Prisoner*. Bill went to Atlanta, where he found Tupper sitting in a waiting area wearing a curly-haired wig. Tupper then calmly autographed all the books Bill brought. In 1986, James Earl Ray, imprisoned at Tennessee's maximum-security prison near Pikeville, had sent Saussy a postcard asking him to help write his biography. Saussy went to see Ray and concluded that Ray was a sacrificial victim and innocent of having killed Martin Luther King Jr. He decided to edit Ray's book. Many people think Saussy wrote the entire book, as the language and philosophical thoughts expressed in it were too sophisticated to have been written by Ray and sounded like Tupper. Saussy admitted to writing part of the book and having edited the rest of it. He thought about claiming credit for "as told to" status, but decided that Ray had been taken advantage of by enough mercenaries that he didn't want to do the same thing. After Saussy published *Tennessee Waltz* in 1987, Ray disavowed certain parts of it and sued him.

After their April meeting at Hartsfield International Airport, Bill heard nothing further from Tupper for several months. He told a staff writer for *The Atlanta Journal* and *The Atlanta Constitution* that fall, "The less I know about Tupper's whereabouts, the better."[46]

In October 1986, Tupper Saussy wrote a letter to the *Nashville Banner* from an unknown location. In it he argued that the Sixth Circuit Court's denial of his appeal put at stake not only his, but also the freedom of all Americans. Tupper wrote that the Sixth Circuit's opinion, if left unchallenged, "would enable prosecutors to bypass the constitutional safeguards of grand jury and sworn affidavit of probable cause in hauling off to jail any citizen targeted for harboring ideas disagreeable to the powers that be. This procedure was the method by which Adolph Hitler gained control, and it is today the rule in the Soviet Union and all totalitarian states. As the court's opinion declares that there has never been a case similar to this, my attorneys this week filed a petition for rehearing *en banc*, which means the entire roster of the Sixth Circuit judges would hear the case. If that is denied, we shall proceed to the United States Supreme Court." Tupper ended by saying, "My wife and family join me in expressing our gratitude to those in the community who have been so supportive of us throughout this experience."[47]

Meanwhile, Freddie didn't feel like anyone was supporting her. The tax evasion conviction, the pressure she had been living under, the glare of publicity that fell on her children, and the fact that Tupper was on the run were too much for her. She successfully filed for divorce, and retained custody of their two children. She next sold their house in Sewanee that had been abandoned since Tupper disappeared, and the building down the street where Tupper published his anti-government newsletter, the *Main Street Journal*, that had ceased regular publication in April. Susan Binkley bought the building to house her Blue Chair Restaurant and looked at the house several times. One day after going through the house, she and her husband Clay went to their car when Susan decided to take another look. She walked back to the house and entered the kitchen, where she noticed a candle burning on the kitchen table. She had not seen the candle when she was in the room a few minutes earlier. This spooked her and the Binkleys did not make an offer.[48]

In November 1987, Tupper's brother, Bill Saussy, general manager of Saint Andrews Press, submitted an article to *The Tennessean*. In it, he offered some corrections about an article

The Tennessean had written about Tupper the previous week. He said Tupper co-founded the Saint Andrews Press and then formed a corporation to protect it and give it legal status. "Therefore, Tupper did not himself publish *Tennessee Waltz* by James Earl Ray. Saint Andrews Press did. Tupper edited the book and wrote a foreword and afterword."[49]

By 1989, Bill Saussy had moved from Sewanee to the Florida Keys and Tupper's second wife, Freddie, had returned to Puerto Rico with their two teenaged sons.[50]

Every blue moon, someone would allegedly see Tupper. In June 1988, Saussy was sighted in California. According to Deputy Federal Marshal Wendell Whaley of Chattanooga, Saussy was wearing a wig and a collar, "passing himself off as a minister representing a diocese in the British West Indies." The tip enabled investigators to find a motor home they believed Saussy was driving and some gold and silver coins, but no Saussy. Whaley said that Saussy had obtained a false birth certificate that enabled him to get a driver's license and that he had the help across the country of other folks "sympathetic to his cause." He said that Tupper's high intelligence also made capture difficult because "he's got an idea about how we're trying to locate him, so he's ready for us." Whaley predicted that "sooner or later" the government would capture Saussy.[51]

Saussy would later say that his life on the run "was not the miserable existence one's imagination is prone to depict. I was never without a keyboard or music. If you had walked through Rainier Center Mall in Seattle's downtown during the summer of 1988, you'd have seen me playing Bach's 'Goldberg Variations' on the Steinway grand that sits in the atrium." Tupper added, "I was blowing about as the spirit moved me."[52] He said he lived a relatively normal life in California with his nutritionist girlfriend Nancy. Since nobody seemed interested in finding him, he took off the hairpiece he was wearing and spent time "as a religious counselor, pianist, computer handy man, homeless person, Bible student, and patron of public and university libraries from Seattle to Key West to Nashville."[53] He played piano in various nightclubs, and was in Washington, D.C., when the Statue of Freedom was removed from the dome of the U.S. Capitol. Some of his close associates knew his identity. Others did not. One of those who did was a fellow fugitive who got caught and gave federal agents information that would lead to Saussy's capture.[54]

During his California years on the lam, Tupper became friends with some unorthodox religious leaders and explored various faiths that were far from mainstream. Saussy's friend from Sewanee days, Patrick Anderson, reflected on the sad situation Tupper had gotten himself in, "I think it's tragic he got off on this political kick. He is, in my opinion, a totally non-political person. He was living in a fantasy world. I don't think he had any sense of what he was doing or what the consequences would be."[55] Tupper maintained telephone contact with his family and occasionally with his first wife Lola, who had remarried.[56] He seldom spoke to friends in Nashville or Chattanooga.

In the meantime, the Montgomery Bell Academy and Nashville communities became excited in 1990 when Tom Schulman, MBA Class of 1968, received an Oscar for the best original screenplay for his film *Dead Poets Society,* in which Robin Williams played the lead role. When Schulman was a sophomore at MBA, he had studied English under Sam Pickering Jr., who was a graduate of MBA, the University of the South, Princeton University, and the University of Cambridge. Schulman based the lead role in the screenplay on Pickering. The movie continues to bring MBA favorable national publicity. Pickering later told me that many of the unusual mannerisms he used in his MBA classroom were learned when he studied under Tupper Saussy as an MBA senior in 1958 and 1959.

Lola Haun French died in Key West on October 26, 1995 at age fifty-five.[57] Upon hearing of Lola's death, Mary Walton Caldwell expressed surprise that she had not died earlier as she lived life "hard." Lola and Tupper's daughter Vana also has had a difficult life, suffering for many years with a drug problem that started when she was in high school. Recovered, she was working, in 2009, to help other addicts. Tupper and Lola's son Haun, who inherited Tupper's brains, has had a spectacular academic career. In 2009, he was Bird White Housum Professor of Comparative Literature and International studies and chairman of the Council on East Asian Studies at Yale University. When he was being recruited to Yale from Stanford University, someone on the search committee thought Haun, who had a bachelor's degree from Duke University and a post-graduate degree from Yale, might be Chinese. Paul Freidman, another search committee member, who had earlier taught at Vanderbilt, knew otherwise. Paul said, "He's not Chinese. He's from Nashville."

In 1996, old Nashville friends hoped Tupper would elude capture forever. As one prominent socialite said, "Darling, he is one of us." Mary Walton Caldwell reflected on his brilliance. She recalled that, during the 1970s, he "was a guest soloist with the Nashville Symphony" and that the Baldwin Piano Company had named him "most promising young pianist of the year." She thought they gave him a free piano. Many admirers felt that he was so multi-talented, he had difficulty focusing on one thing for very long. Most agreed he was his own worst enemy.[58]

On November 14, 1997, ten years, seven months and four days after Tupper became a fugitive from justice, a U.S. Marshal arrested him as he began to drive away from the Los Angeles home he shared with Nancy. Suddenly, two cars blocked him in. A Marshal got out of one of the cars, held up a badge, and asked him if he was Frederick Tupper Saussy III. "No," Saussy replied, "I am not."[59] The Marshal was not fooled. Tupper would be held in California for return to Tennessee, where he was expected to face additional charges for his decade on the run.

After his capture, Saussy spent five months in solitary confinement, once again in the federal penitentiary in Atlanta. There, he spent his time reading the Bible and other material in the library. He hated the fact that there was no piano. This was the longest period of time in his life that he could not play the piano. In the spring of

1998, Tupper was transferred to Taft, a low-security prison near Los Angeles where, in May that year, he was choir director, unofficial counselor to fellow inmates and prison minister. He was delighted to find that he had access to a piano at Taft. Consequently, he gave voice, composition, and piano lessons to several promising inmates. His former attorney Lowell Becraft predicted in May 1998 that Tupper would probably have to spend about twenty months in prison. "I'm spending my time productively," Tupper said. "It's a marvelous experience. The fields are ripe for harvest, and there is a lot of harvesting going on." Although Tupper didn't appear to be repentant, he seemed to be planning to live a law-abiding life when he was released. He also had misgivings about again butting heads with federal authority. "I had been reduced to an angry, frustrated voice that had no hope of ever being clearly brokered through channels of information most people trusted. Worse, I was beginning to discover that my approach was all wrong," he said.

When he was released from prison, Tupper remained in Santa Monica, California, living with Nancy until her children complained.[60] He then moved to his hometown of Statesboro, Georgia, where his sister lived. Unsatisfied with living in a small, Deep South town of 25,000 people, Tupper began to visit Nashville, where he stayed with Jack and Lynn May. After moving to Nashville in 2005, where he still had many friends, he rented apartment B-4 in Helena Court, an apartment house on Belle Meade Boulevard that was built in 1930. Tupper loved the irony of the fact that his apartment number B-4, pronounced "before," was remindful of the fact that he had once before lived on Belle Meade Boulevard.

Once Tupper found his footing back in the Nashville world, he seemed to recreate the existence he had known more than thirty years earlier. He forged a friendship again with restaurateur Joe Ledbetter, even becoming the creative force behind the logo for Ledbetter's new restaurant on West End. On more than one occasion, after Tupper's death, Joe lamented how mad he was at Tupper for dying and depriving Nashville of his creative genius. Brad Gioia, MBA's headmaster, recalled in 2009 the two or three occasions when he knew of Tupper's performance at a local music scene, and regretted not having ventured out those evenings to hear him. Soon after Tupper's death, Brad listened to a wonderful program on

This photo of Frederick Tupper Saussy III was taken in 2006 at Dorothy Earthman's house. Photo courtesy of Haun Saussy.

Nashville Public Radio during which they played a collection of Tupper's best music. Brad told me in 2009 that one of his favorite times in MBA history was the moment the school recognized Tom Schulman as the Distinguished Alumnus. After Tom gave a wonderful response, Brad introduced him to Tupper, who, as mentioned earlier, was "one of the great inspirations behind the film and antics of Mr. Keating." One of Brad's prized possessions is a portrait Tupper painted of Brad's wife, Minna. Brad had seen several of Tupper's works of art at a local art gallery and, upon learning that he was once again painting portraits, sought him out to do the piece. Tupper came by the Gioia home late one afternoon to take photographs of Minna. A few months later, a beautiful portrait arrived. Brad made the point that Tupper ended his life in a wonderful way the last few years he was in Nashville. "He returned to the foundations of creativity through some work in the advertising world. He reconnected briefly at MBA. He performed some music to packed houses and he did some painting. For a brief time Tupper Saussy's genius and artistic spark shined again."

Tupper was also very interested in religion at this point in his life. Specifically, he was a convert to numerology, the study of the occult significance of numbers. Of course, none of this made sense to Lynn and Jack May. At some point, Tupper asked Lynn whom he should date. She suggested Tish Fort, who, by then, went only by her first name "Tish." Tupper said he thought he would ask out the "Widow Earthman." Tupper and Dorothy enjoyed each other's company and became constant companions. They were frequently seen at upscale Nashville parties and enjoyed going to house parties at Beersheba, where Dorothy had a second home. Later, when asked by Lynn how he and Dorothy were getting along, Tupper said, "The Earthman widow is crazy about me."

The first time I realized Tupper was back in Nashville was one evening when Irene and I saw him at a party Chloe Lenderman gave at her home on Sunnyside. Although I had not seen Tupper in two decades, it quickly dawned on me who he was. Later that evening, I told Tupper about all the changes at MBA since he left Nashville and offered to take him on a campus tour. He accepted and seemed excited about seeing all the physical changes at the school.

Early on Friday morning, March 16, 2007, Lynn May received a phone call from an extremely distraught Dorothy Earthman, who wanted to speak to Jack. When Lynn told her that Jack was not there, Dorothy screamed that Tupper was dead and that she needed Lynn to come to Tupper's apartment immediately. Dressed only in her pajamas, Lynn threw on a robe and drove to the Helena Court where she found Dorothy alone with Tupper's body, which was impeccably clothed in a sports jacket and tie. He was seated at his computer with his head back. While Dorothy wept, Lynn called 911 and soon the police, the fire department, and the coroner were there. Assuming that Lynn had spent the night there because she still had on her nightclothes, the officers asked her all sorts of questions that she was incapable of answering. She did learn from Dorothy that she had come to Tupper's apartment just before she called Lynn because, the night before, when she and Tupper had planned to go to

Bricktops for dinner, he never appeared. Concerned that something might be wrong, Dorothy came to his apartment and found him dead. He had suffered a fatal heart attack.

Tupper's untimely death came only a week before he was to give a concert celebrating the release of his newest CD and first album in thirty-eight years, *The Chocolate Orchid Piano Bar*. This piece features Tupper alone at the piano, singing original compositions dating from the 1960s to 2007. The CD captures the man in all his voices: romantic, anguished, mocking, and wistful.[61]

Tupper's son Haun learned about his father's death after his Aunt Lynda left an e-mail message that said, "Call me." Under the subject line were the words "your father." Haun wondered, "Was he about to get married, the romantic seventy-year-old? Had he invented a new form of currency? Had a small island nation invited him to be their king? As Haun went downstairs "imagining these pleasant and not unlikely scenarios," the phone rang. He learned that his father had died. A week later, Haun recalled what it was like growing up the son of Tupper Saussy.

"When you were with him, you always felt that exciting things were just about to happen. Parents are a child's whole world, and the world with Tupper was unpredictable, weightless, charmed. It would not have surprised me to encounter talking animals, philosophical pirates, or a teenager named William Shakespeare any more than it would to meet a contrarian's insight, a pun, or the portrait of a crushed bag executed with attention worthy of a dowager empress. Such things were the stuff of daily life with Tupper. The elements of his world never went to sleep or hardened into rigid order; they were always up for recombination and surprise. Our house rang with music, laughter, and talk, as did every house he inhabited."[62]

Tupper Saussy's death robbed Nashville of one of the city's most talented and clever men, someone who exuded energy, charm and wit, though not always appropriately directed. His sphere of interest was far ranging and his worst enemy was indeed himself. At the visitation before his funeral, a man Lynn May had never seen before asked her if Tupper had any needle marks on his neck when he died. When she said that she never heard of anything like that, he said that the U.S. Government murdered him. That figures. At the funeral, one of Tupper's old musician friends said to Haun, "Your dad lived his own life to the fullest, and (the lives of) six other guys in China, too." Later, Haun mused about, "How much better it would have been for my father if he had left the IRS alone."

Chapter 11

Margaret Lindsley Warden
1904–2007

In 1986, when Margaret Lindsley Warden learned, probably at The Downtown Presbyterian Church where we were all members, that our son Morgan was going to Princeton, she asked Irene and me to do her a favor. She wanted us, whenever we visited Morgan at the school, to go over to Nassau Hall and see if the portrait of her great-grandfather, Philip Lindsley, was still prominently displayed. Lindsley was acting president of the College of New Jersey, now Princeton University, before accepting the presidency of Nashville's struggling Cumberland College in 1824. Margaret explained that her agreement was that she would give the portrait to Princeton on the condition that it would always hang in a prominent place in Nassau Hall. If we found that not to be the case, she instructed us to bring the portrait home. Irene and I dutifully went to Nassau Hall each time we visited Morgan. When he graduated in 1990, I reported to Margaret that we had fulfilled our charge and assured her that the portrait's location seemed secure.

I've known Margaret all my life.[1]
Margaret Lindsley Warden, the daughter of Ann Dickinson

Lindsley and Carl Warden, was born in Battle Creek, Michigan, on January 11, 1904. Her mother was the youngest daughter of Sallie McGavock and John Berrien Lindsley, the second chancellor of the University of Nashville. Her great grandfathers were Jacob McGavock and Philip Lindsley.

Margaret's father, Carl Warden, came to Nashville from somewhere up North with letters of introduction as a physician to Dr. John Berrien Lindsley. He was seeking a milder climate for some respiratory problem and practiced in the large McGavock-Lindsley home on Spruce Street where Margaret's mother lived. After being in Nashville for a while, Mr. Warden accepted a position with Phelps Sanitarium in Battle Creek, Michigan, where Margaret was born. He "preferred one of his patients" to Margaret's mother, however, and left them. Mr. Warden was never to see Margaret again except for once when, as a child, she was taken to see him. After that, Mr. Warden's name was seldom mentioned in the Lindsley household.

When she was a child, Margaret's aunts and uncles took turns supporting her and her mother. The place where they boarded the longest was at Miss Eliza Douglas' home just up the hill from Renraw, the home of her aunt, Margaret Lindsley Warner, and her husband, Percy Warner, in East Nashville.

In 1910, Margaret started attending Sunday School at the First Presbyterian Church, where five generations of her family had preceded her. Her great-grandfather Jacob McGavock's pew, Number One Hundred and Eleven, where Margaret and her mother sat, still has his name on the brass plate. As so many children did, Margaret memorized the Shorter Catechism and earned a New Testament. Her Sunday School teacher was Mrs. Verner Moore Lewis.

Margaret's education was a classical one that included reading the best literature and listening to the best music. She attended musical performances in the Ryman Auditorium with her mother, and became acquainted with the best opera plots, arias, and the great singers, her favorite being Amelita Galli-Curci.

In 1913, Margaret entered Ward Seminary in the second or third grade. That fall, she and her mother moved to 1806 East Belmont Circle because the Percy Warners had moved from Renraw on Gallatin Pike to Royal Oaks on Harding Road. Margaret would live at 1806 East Belmont Circle for the next seventy-four years.

Margaret's first exposure to horses came when she and some fellow students at Ward-Belmont (Ward having merged with Belmont College for Young Women) went to a weekend camp owned by Walter Parmer at Edenwold. There she and her friends took turns riding an unfit horse around an oval track.

Dances were a pain for Margaret as she was not pretty and not particularly interested in boys. Often, Merrill Moore, an MBA student who realized that his fellow students shied away from her, looked after her. Margaret had her first and only date with Dudley Gale, a handsome young man, whom Margaret's friends said had a reputation for being a bit risqué. He took her to a movie because he wanted her opinion on the pedigree of a horse. He also did not make a pass at Margaret. No one ever did.

At Ward-Belmont, Margaret enjoyed the music department led by F. Arthur Henkel, who later conducted the Nashville Symphony Orchestra. The concerts were outstanding. Margaret also enjoyed art and Latin. She graduated from the high school in 1920 and from the junior college in 1922. At that graduation, she wore her Aunt Louise's shoes and a borrowed dress, sort of lacy. Because the shoes were too large, she had to clutch with her toes to keep them on.

About 1921, Margaret joined the Girls' Cotillion Club, but only because her aunts Miss Louise Lindsley and Margaret (Mrs. Percy) Warner insisted that she do so. She did, however, add "damn cotillion" to her dues check stub.

In 1922, Margaret enrolled at George Peabody College, where she loved art history and poetry, including that of Emily Dickinson. Peabody had a historical link to the University of Nashville, where both her grandfather and great-grandfather, John Berrien and Philip Lindsley, had been chancellors.

After graduation, in 1924, Margaret considered becoming a teacher but decided not to when told that beginning teachers were given the roughest students. A few months later, in January 1925, Margaret wrote her first column about horses in *The Nashville Tennessean*. She was invited to do so by Colonel Luke Lea, who owned the paper and who married Margaret's first cousin Mary Louise Warner. Because Margaret did not own a typewriter or much of anything else, she dictated her articles to a public stenographer at the Maxwell House Hotel. Because she had no stature as a horse writer, Margaret used a pseudonym, "Cade," the name of a famous English thoroughbred foaled in 1734. She knew that famous horse writers, such as John Hervey, often wrote under pseudonyms. His pen name was "Salvator."

Proud of Margaret's accomplishments as a competent writer, Aunt Louise, who was closer to Margaret than was her niece's own mother, kept a scrapbook of all Margaret's columns, almost forgetting her disappointment over Margaret's failure to make the grade in society.

In the 1920s, with help from Aunt Louise, Margaret attended and covered some of the great national horse shows, including the International Livestock Exposition in Chicago, the Chicago Riding Club Horse Show, and the National Horse Show in New York's Madison Square Garden. For the riding club show, Margaret stayed at the Del Prado Hotel and rode a crowded and dirty but cheap streetcar to the event. Once, Aunt Louise took Margaret to Lexington to see the great studs: Himyar, Hinata, Shandon, Donegal, and Elmendorf. There, Margaret wrangled an invitation to meet Miss Elizabeth Dangerfield, manager of Man o' War, the world's greatest thoroughbred. She also saw Bourbon King, sire of the American saddle horse breed. On another visit to Lexington she met the editor of *The Thoroughbred Record*. By then, Margaret had a small typewriter with a green ribbon, her favorite color.

Margaret's first horse was Emma, a one-eyed black horse rented from Derby Stables on Nashville's First Avenue. She would rent her for one dollar an hour. A groom would bring the horse up Villa Place to 1806 East Belmont Circle saddled and bridled. Margaret would ride with Ellen Stokes to Love Circle and across open fields south of Vanderbilt. In 1928, Margaret began working at the Presbyterian Book Store at 711 Church Street for fifteen dollars a week. Her Aunt Louise snorted, "Working to support a horse." Margaret would walk to work and ride the streetcar home.

Sarah Berry exposed Margaret to the opera when they traveled together to Chicago. Sarah agreed to go to the horse show if Margaret would go with her to the Chicago Opera Company's performance.

During the late 1920s, Margaret visited her first cousin, Sadie Warner Frazer, and her husband George Frazer in Washington. There she visited Fort Myer, where she witnessed cavalry drills and went to area racetracks. An indefatigable walker, Margaret loved to walk in Rock Creek Park and at the zoo, to tour public buildings and visit second-hand bookstores.

In June 1928, Margaret enjoyed a European trip with a Ward-Belmont group. While in England, she visited Newmarket and the studs in that area. On her last day in England, she went alone to the Aintree Race Course, site of the Grand National Steeplechase.

The Southern Grasslands Hunt and Racing Foundation purchased Sumner County's Fairvue mansion in 1929. They planned to renovate the house as the foundation's headquarters. The idea was to have steeplechase racing, polo, horse breeding, and general farming there. With grandiose plans, the foundation bought eighty farms between Hendersonville and Gallatin and consolidated these into a twenty-eight square-mile holding. The Inaugural Steeplechase was held May 19, 1930, the Monday after the Kentucky Derby. The first International Steeplechase was held December 6, 1930, the day after a big ball. *The Nashville Tennessean* reported that few Tennesseans had been present. On November 8, 1931, two days after the second International Steeplechase, Caldwell and Company failed. Grassland staggered on until it was put in receivership March 7, 1932. Late in the decade, ride-a-thons sprang up in Middle Tennessee only to be suspended for the duration of the war. In 1939, Margaret began writing a Sunday column for *The Nashville Tennessean* titled "Horse Sense."

Margaret's routine during the late 1940s was to spend two weeks in New York City going to the Metropolitan Opera and seeing horse shows and attractions before returning home by train. The rest of the year she was chief reporter and commentator for equestrian events in the Nashville area, including covering the Tennessee Walking Horse Celebration in Shelbyville in late August and the Brentwood Horse Show sponsored for many years by the Robertson Academy PTA. She also covered the field trials in October for the Fox Hunters Association. The postwar years were happy and busy ones as horse shows were usually at night, often thirty to fifty miles from Nashville. *The Nashville Tennessean* reimbursed her for food and lodging and she invariably rode with someone else.

On the art scene, Margaret was a volunteer for the Nashville Museum of Art, often given the job of unpacking, hanging, and repacking art work for traveling art exhibits. She also was active in the Nashville Opera Guild during the decade that led her editors at *The Nashville Tennessean* to assign her to cover concerts at the Ryman and at War Memorial Auditorium, including ones by Nelson Eddy and James Melton.

Margaret's happiness in the 1940s was tempered by the death of her Aunt Louise Lindsley, her adopted parent, friend, and mentor. Of course, it never had occurred to Aunt Louise to get Margaret an automobile, as this was considered inappropriate for genteel ladies of her generation. It also was unseemly for a lady to drive herself to Middle Tennessee towns for horse shows without a chaperone. Mary (Mrs. Lambert) Campbell would, in many ways, take Aunt Louise's place.

In the early 1950s, Coleman Harwell offered to talk to Margaret about a full-time job at *The Nashville Tennessean*. This would have improved Margaret's finances and given her retirement benefits she did not have as a part-time employee. She declined because the equestrian world, not the newspaper world, was her cup of tea. She was afraid that, as a full-time employee, she would not have the time or the energy to do what she enjoyed most.

After writing her Horse Sense column for *The Nashville Tennessean* for fifteen years, Margaret founded a pleasure horse show in 1952 that she called the Horse Sense Riding Tournament. One hundred twenty-five horses and ponies participated in the first event on Labor Day in Edwin Warner Park. *The Nashville Tennessean* sponsored the second annual event in 1953. In 1954, the Olympic Three-Day Event trials were added to the tournament. These were the first Three-Day trials ever held away from Fort Riley, Kansas. The purpose of the trials was to judge a squad of six horses and riders from which a team of three would be selected to represent the United States at the Pan-American Games in Mexico City in 1955. Margaret was the general director of the event. The Horse Sense Riding Tournament had more than twenty divisions in the 1960s.

In 1953 there was only one Pony Club in the United States that was a branch of the original Pony Club in England; it was in Maryland. Margaret wrote the chief promoter of the club asking permission to organize a Pony Club in Nashville. Permission was granted and the Middle Tennessee Pony Club became the first affiliate, chartered by the brand new United States Pony Club. The charters of both were dated February 1954. Margaret, Ruth Kinnard, and Cynthia Schell got it started; they set up a card table at the Grassland School Fall Horse Show. On the table there was a sign reading, "Join the Pony Club." Twenty-three children paid the one dollar membership fee and the club was off and running. Guilford Dudley Jr. was particularly helpful, including allowing the club to meet at his Northumberland Stud on Harding Place. In 1955, the MTPC made an impressive showing at the first USPC National Rally in Chester County, Pennsylvania. Of the eleven teams in the "C" division, the MTPC took fifth in the finals, having been first in dressage and tied for first in jumping. The president of the USPC said the MTPC was "by far the best riding team in the meeting."

One of Margaret's many legacies was her leadership in the successful effort to save Belle Meade Plantation. Margaret was a charter member of the APTA (the Association for the Preservation of Tennessee Antiquities) and was elected corresponding secretary at the first annual luncheon meeting in January 1952. In 1953, the APTA acquired two significant properties: The Ramsey House in Knoxville and Belle Meade. The acquisition of Belle Meade stemmed from its threatened purchase by the Belle Meade United Methodist Church as the site for their new sanctuary. In 1953, Mrs. Guilford Dudley Jr., one of the APTA leaders, led the effort that persuaded the legislature to purchase Belle Meade for $125,000.

In the 1960s, Margaret was chairman of the Carriage House Committee at Belle Meade. Every Sunday, after worship services at The Downtown Presbyterian Church, Martha Lindsey, a close friend who was also unmarried, would drive Margaret to Belle Meade. Margaret would take her lunch with her: a slice of bread and an apple. She would open up the carriage house for visitors. At 5 PM she would lock up and walk to the bus stop at Leake Avenue and Belle Meade Boulevard and ride the city bus to Fairfax and West End. There she would get off and walk east on Fairfax to her home on East Belmont Circle. Margaret loved walking all her life and would often walk to her job at *The Nashville Tennessean*. If a gentleman offered her a ride, she would quickly glance to see if she knew him. If she did not, she would neither look at him nor answer.

Once Colonel Paul Downing, an authority on restoring carriages, visited Belle Meade. Margaret tried to learn all she could from him. Later, he invited her to a carriage meeting up East, including spending one or two nights at his home. When Margaret didn't answer his letter, he called her to inquire why. Margaret said, "Your wife has not invited me so I cannot accept your invitation."

What Margaret remembered most clearly about Belle Meade happened during her term as chairman of the Nashville Chapter of the APTA. Open warfare developed between the APTA and the APTA's Nashville Chapter over Belle Meade's involvement with Orrin Wickersham "Wick" June's Historic Sites Federation, of which there were three other members: Travellers Rest, Oaklands, and Cragfont. The APTA leadership strenuously objected to Belle Meade's involvement. When the Nashville Chapter APTA sold a breakfront and a chandelier that were not of the era that Belle Meade was portraying without permission of the parent board, the president of the APTA fired Margaret and the other members of the thirty-person board, including Helen (Mrs. Robert) Cheek; Guilford Dudley Jr.; Stanley Horn; Hortense (Mrs. O. H.) Ingram; Ed Potter; Vernon Sharp; and Bill Waller. It took Belle Meade a long time to recover from this 1971 loss of top-flight leadership. Later, when my wife and I got involved in resurrecting Belle Meade, Margaret was a stalwart supporter. It was her research in 1990 that led her to discover that, of the fifty-three Thoroughbred Horses of the Year between 1937 and 1989, forty-six were descended from Belle Meade's great sire, Bonnie Scotland.

When First Presbyterian Church voted in 1954 to move to Oak Hill, Margaret stood with the minority group that bought the old sanctuary downtown in 1955 and established The Downtown Presbyterian Church. For her entire life, she had gone to church there, just as her McGavock and Lindsley ancestors had. When she was a student at Ward Seminary, most of the student body walked in formation to First Presbyterian from the school on Eighth Avenue. Along the way, idle boys would heckle the girls calling them "Ward's Ducks." Once at church, the girls sat in a group in a section reserved for them. Margaret helped the new church become established and once even painted the wrought iron fence surrounding it. On that occasion, she took off her white gloves.

During the 1960s, Margaret established inter-school riding tour-naments and a Middle Tennessee Pony Club horse quiz game based on the standard spelling bee. The Quiz Bee was adopted by the USPC in the 1970s. Margaret even acquired a few thoroughbreds. She had longed for a horse or a pony from her childhood. Through the encouragement of a cousin, Peggy Dickinson Fleming, Margaret bought three thoroughbreds: a stallion, a mare, and a gelding. Margaret called them "three castoffs of a noble breed." She did not stay in the business long.

Margaret was a founding member of the Metropolitan Historical Commission (MHC). She served as secretary from 1966 until 1973, when she became MHC chairman. In that role, she conceived the idea of establishing an architectural awards program. Following a pattern established by the National Trust for Historic Preservation, the architectural awards program was inaugurated as part of Historic Preservation Week in May. The Metro Council recognized the worth of what Margaret had started and granted sufficient funds to the Metro Historical Commission to employ an executive director. May Dean Eberling, who for six years had been an outstanding staff member of the Tennessee Historical Commission, was highly recom-mended. Her outstanding tenure at the Metro Historical Commission lasted until 1982. In January 1983, Ann Reynolds, another admirer and friend of Margaret's, succeeded May Dean Eberling as executive director.

Sometime in the 1980s, I received a phone call from Dr. Bill Troutt, a friend of mine who was president of Belmont University. He asked me if I would help him convince Margaret to sell her house at 1806 East Belmont Circle to the university, as they needed her two lots to build a new building. Having known and respected Margaret all my adult life, and realizing that she had lived in her house since 1913, I declined, thinking she should not have to move at that point in her life.

Margaret learned about the university's plans from Margaret White Greenlee, a librarian at Belmont who heard, at a faculty meeting, that Belmont intended to acquire the property. Greenlee passed the information on to Margaret Warden, possibly through her brother, John White. Margaret was frightened. John, whose grand-mother, Margaret Lindsley (Mrs. John O.) White, was Margaret

Lindsley Warden's sister, agreed to help Margaret negotiate with Belmont. He had been in the real estate business, while Margaret had no real estate experience. John negotiated an arrangement under which Belmont would acquire only the lot on which Margaret's four-square, two-story house stood, while the adjoining lot, which faced Acklen, would remain Margaret's. On it, Belmont would build for her a house as nearly identical as possible to the one the university intended to demolish. Because the 1906 house had been constructed of molded concrete block material no longer available, the new house was built of red brick chosen by Margaret. Other changes were made, but the university worked hard to build a house that Margaret liked, even graciously imitating the diamond pattern on the front windows. Because Margaret did not want to change her mailing address, Nashvillian Marvin Runyon, then Postmaster General of the United States, made an exception and left the address as 1806 Belmont Circle. The university even moved Margaret's two pet Golden Sebright Bantam hens that Margaret had lovingly cared for since the 1970s. They also disassembled the very large four-piece bedroom suite, a gift of Margaret's cousins in Louisville, Kentucky, and moved it in a responsible manner. Because parking is usually a problem on Acklen Avenue and East Belmont Circle, the university gave Margaret a reserved parking space in the surface parking lot directly across the street from her house. When the day came to tear down the old house, Margaret could not bear to watch it "bite the dust," so she spent two nights with her cousin Mary Louise Tidwell. When she returned the old lot was clean as a whistle, mitigating somewhat her sorrow at losing an old friend. In turn for paying for Margaret's new house, the university would gain title to it upon Margaret's death. After Margaret moved in 1988, Belmont's presidents, Bill Troutt and Bob Fisher, were very considerate of Margaret, often visiting her.

About this time, Margaret made a new friend, Mary Ella Burke, whom Margaret described as "blue-ribbon class." This friendship helped Margaret with her transition as did putting together a birthday celebration at Mount Olivet Cemetery for Felix Grundy, Margaret's great-great-grandfather. Chief speakers on the occasion were cousin John Warner White and Senator Douglas Henry Jr. Over the years, Margaret also arranged birthday celebrations at Mount

Margaret Lindsley Warden in her home. Photo courtesy of
Mary Ella Burke.

Margaret Lindsley Warden. Photo courtesy of Mary Ella Burke.

Olivet for Colonel Randal McGavock, who was killed at Raymond, Mississippi, in 1863.

In 1990, Margaret was named the recipient of the Tennessee Horse Council's Horseperson of the Year Award. Later, the award was named after Margaret.

Many times, Mark Brown, executive director of Belmont Mansion, and Bill Trout, Belmont's president, would look out on Belmont Boulevard and marvel at the sight of the diminutive Margaret, wearing no-nonsense flat shoes, a little hat, white gloves, and a plain dress, as she walked from the Hillsboro bus line to her home east of the campus. I would occasionally see her, too, wearing the same attire, sitting upright on a bench at the bus stop next to the Newspaper Printing Corporation office on Broad Street patiently waiting for the city bus to take her home from work. It was a pleasure for me to circle back and give her a ride home.

On June 24, 1994, Margaret retired from *The Tennessean* at age ninety. The announcement came in the paper the following Monday. It said that she had outlasted numerous editors and many techno-logical changes, including going from a manual typewriter with a green ribbon to the computer. For fifty-five years she had turned out her Horse Sense column, and had been writing articles about once a week since 1939.

Three months later, nearly one hundred people attended a Middle Tennessee Pony Club reunion and dinner in a tent on the south side of the Steeplechase stable. The event was in honor of Margaret Lindsley Warden for her lifetime of supporting equestrian causes. Margaret tried to deflect credit to Ruth Kinnard and Cynthia Schell for lifting the first affiliate of the new United States Pony Club off the ground. When Margaret died, she still had about thirty congratulatory letters she received on that occasion. Margaret said at that affair or at some other time late in her life, "I couldn't make show horses any showier; I couldn't make race horses any faster, but I would try to promote better horsemanship at the grass-roots level."

Margaret wrote her autobiography, *Life Has Been Very Kind to Me,* in 2000. She dedicated it to "the memory of Louise Grundy Lindsley, my aunt, my strong, loving friend, and parent by adop-tion." John Seigenthaler wrote a charming foreword to the book, in which he spoke of Margaret's relationships in *The Tennessean* newsroom with staff members not half her age who didn't know quite what to think of her.

The title Margaret chose for the book is interesting and ironic, since she did not have an easy life. She did have a generous nature and contributed enormously to Nashville and the equestrian world. We will all cherish and remember her for the rest of our lives.

Not long after writing her autobiography, Margaret's health failed. Fortunately, her nurses, Mary Belle Rutledge and later Brenda Evans and her family, gave Margaret splendid care.

In the summer of 2006, when Margaret was still alert but bedridden, Mary Ella Burke sat beside her and the two friends alternatively quoted to each other, from memory, the stanzas of Alfred Lloyd Tennyson's "Crossing the Bar."

> Sunset and evening star,
> And one clear call for me!
> And may there be no moaning of the bar
> When I put out to sea,
>
> But such a tide as moving seems asleep,
> Too full for sound and foam,
> When that which drew from out the boundless deep
> Turns again home.
>
> Twilight and evening bell,
> And after that the dark!
> And may there be no sadness of farewell,
> When I embark;
>
> For tho' from out our bourne of Time and Place
> The flood may bear me far,
> I hope to see my Pilot face to face
> When I have crossed the bar.

Margaret Lindsley Warden died November 24, 2007, at the age of one hundred and three. A memorial service was held for her at The Downtown Presbyterian Church, where I gave the eulogy. Margaret willed her remains to the Vanderbilt Medical School. Nineteen months later, I got a call from May Dean Eberling, a distant relative of Margaret's and co-executor of her estate. May Dean asked me to speak at the interment of Margaret's ashes at Mt. Olivet Cemetery. In our conversation, May Dean mentioned that Bill Coke was going to dig the grave. I told May Dean that I was going to be out of town that weekend and could not speak. I also asked why in the world Bill was digging the grave. May Dean said that the Mt. Olivet Cemetery people wanted $900 to dig the grave and furnish a tent and chairs. Knowing that Margaret would not have wanted to waste $900 on a small hole, May Dean and Mary Ella decided not to have a tent or chairs and to dig the grave themselves or at least to have Bill do so. It turned out that Mary Ella's son dug the grave and Margaret's ashes were buried there in the little box in which Vanderbilt Medical School had returned her ashes. Senator Douglas Henry Jr. made appropriate remarks. Margaret, always extremely frugal, would have been pleased.

Chapter 12

Ellen Stokes More Wemyss
1895–2001

O ne of Ellen Wemyss's favorite historic houses was Cragfont, a handsome stone house built by General James Winchester in about 1802. Ellen was always on the forefront of those making sure this house was maintained and open to the public. Although my own historic interests were in Davidson County, I always responded with a gift when Ellen called on me to help. I did so because of my great respect for her. She was quite a special lady.

⎯⎯✦⎯⎯

Ellen Stokes was born February 9, 1895. Her parents were Nellie Treanor and Walter Stokes, a prominent Nashville attorney. As a young woman, Mrs. Stokes was one of the founders of a literary group, the Query Club, in 1885.[1] The Stokes' original frame house, located three miles south of Nashville on Hillsboro Pike, burned in November of 1897, when Ellen was a toddler. Her mother, with Ellen in her arms, watched the fire with her sons, Tom and Walter, and her husband's nephew, James Frazor Stokes Jr., who lived with them. Mr. Stokes promised Nellie that he would have another house there by the coming of spring. While the new house was under construction, the Stokeses lived for four months with Bessie Shackleford and her family in her commodious two-story, frame house across the Hillsboro Pike. The replacement home, Breezemont was much grander than the frame house and featured a portico and two-story tall Corinthian columns across the front. By spring, it stood on the ground where its predecessor had burned, overlooking Hillsboro Pike to the west and the surrounding countryside. The Stokes's farm extended east to Belmont Boulevard, north to Cedar Lane, and south to the present Stokes Lane. In 1902, when Ellen was seven years old, Jere Baxter's Tennessee Central Railroad built its mainline track circling the city on the south, slicing Mr. Stokes's farm in half.

Ellen had a wonderful childhood. When she was little, she and her two older brothers had an Irish nurse named Bridget. Mrs. Stokes read to her children every day after lunch and played the piano for them every evening.[2] Ellen saw many of the memorable events in Nashville's history, such as the dedication of Union Station on October 9, 1900, when she was five. Ellen recalled the event ninety-five years later. "I rode in a carriage in the parade, got out at the station and went down the iron steps to the trains. My uncle (William L. Granbery) was an attorney for the Pullman Company and made a speech. I cried out, 'There's Uncle Will.' Everybody laughed. I still remember when he drove over to see us one Sunday in a brand new car (a White Steamer)."[3]

Ellen and her two older brothers lived a very wholesome life. She recalled, "We must have climbed every tree within a mile of our house." The children also collected minie balls they found in rainwashed gullies on Montgomery Hill along the north side of the Stokes's farm. Ellen, Tom, Walter Jr. and two cousins rode their ponies to Waverly School when she was in the first grade. Neighbors called them the "Stokes Cavalry." When Ellen was eleven, her aunt, Mayna Treanor Avent, painted her portrait. [4] When she was thirteen, Ellen had typhoid fever, the only major illness she ever had in her life.[5] Ellen attended Sunnyside School, a private school run by Mrs. Lawrence, and made her debut into Nashville society at age eighteen on February 9, 1913. "All the girls I knew had a big party together. We danced; oh, we had a marvelous time."

Ellen's real passion was riding on her black horse C. C., named for C.C. Henderson, a friend of her future husband, E. Livingfield More. A good athlete and tomboy, Ellen, as a child, won two cups for her skill as a rider. By the time she was ten, she rode horseback through today's Green Hills. When she was older, she often rode with Margaret Lindsley Warden, nine years younger, who lived at 1806 East Belmont Circle. Sterling Peyton, a Confederate veteran and good storyteller, kept a dipper and cedar bucket filled with water on the porch of his tollgate house that stood where the Hillsboro fire hall is today.[6] Ellen enjoyed the refreshing water and never gave a thought to the fact that everybody drank out of the same dipper. She and Margaret also enjoyed riding to the top of Love Circle and across the open fields to its east. As was the case with most of her friends, Ellen never went to college.

At age fifteen, undoubtedly without her parents' permission, Ellen rode in an open cockpit plane that landed on a grass strip on what became Hampton Field. A friend, Marie Kuhn, went up first and was so excited she convinced Ellen to do the same. Ellen did not have fifteen dollars with her to pay for the fifteen-minute ride, but the pilot just told her to pay him later. After Marie agreed to watch after "Hell," Ellen's half Great Dane, half bulldog, she climbed aboard. An old country man looking on said, "She shore do look scared." Ellen heard him and said, "She shore is scared." The pilot took off and immediately flew over Ellen's house, which was less than a mile away. Ellen looked down and saw the houseman scrubbing the front walk. In recalling the event in 1980, Ellen said, "We flew over the fairgrounds and circled around the race track and then came back. That was my first flight in an airplane."[7]

Ellen was also excited when John T. Landis, the owner of one of the first cars in town, drove his White Steamer out to the Stokes farm. Ellen reminisced decades later that, "It was like something from Mars to me. I stood in front of it and looked at it and he blew his horn. I was scared to death."[8]

In 1918, Ellen dressed as Joan of Arc in a Red Cross Parade to raise money for the war effort and to honor France's role in World

Miss Ellen Stokes as "Joan of Arc" in the French Independence Day Parade in Nashville on July 14, 1918. Photo from Davidson County Women in the World War 1914–1919 *by Rose Long Gilmore.*

War I. In the parade, she rode astride and wore a costume made by her mother overnight.[9]

The women's suffrage fight in Nashville took place in the hot summer of 1920. Ellen supported the cause enthusiastically and marched in a suffragette parade from downtown to Centennial Park. In 1995, Ellen said, "Women had to fight for their rights and it wasn't an easy job," Later in 1920, she cast her first vote in a presidential election. Ellen voted for the unsuccessful Democratic party nominee, James M. Cox, and his running mate, Franklin Delano Roosevelt. [10]

In 1925, when Ellen was thirty, she married E. Livingfield More, a native Nashvillian who was born in 1867 at Belair, the home of his grandfather, William Nichol, on the Lebanon Turnpike. When asked why she waited so long to marry Livingfield, who was fifty-eight, Ellen said, "I was too busy."

After graduating from St. Paul's School in Concord, New Hampshire, More moved to Montana, where he worked as a cowboy for four years. Returning to Nashville, he was active in the planning of the Tennessee Centennial Exposition. Not long after the Centennial closed, More went to work for the L&N Railroad. There, he was put in charge of building a branch line from Georgiana, Alabama, to Graceville, Florida. This took him to River Falls in Covington County, Alabama, where he acquired controlling interest in a small sawmill. In 1898, he organized the Horse Shoe Lumber Company that cut and rafted long leaf yellow pine lumber to the Gulf of Mexico where it was marketed.

More made his fortune with the Horse Shoe Lumber Company, cutting some 125,000 acres of pine forest in South Alabama. He remained president of the company until it closed in 1929 when the mill was dismantled.[11]

In 1922, More organized the River Falls Power Company which built two hydro-electric dams on the Conecuh River and subsequently provided electricity for nine counties in South Alabama. More was also a director of cotton mills, banks, and fertilizer companies.

For the next nine years, Ellen and Livingfield lived in River Falls, in a beautiful home that was long noted for its Southern charm and hospitality. They were blessed with a son, E. Livingfield "Livy" More Jr., born July 11, 1926. Ellen had the help of two African-American house servants, Emma Griffin and Mary Hobday, who lived in a small house near the "Big House." Both women were state convicts whose services Livingfield had leased from the state. They were also the lifetime beneficiaries of a trust created by Mr. More after he was taken sick late in his life, and, at his request, were pardoned by the Governor of Alabama.[12]

The Mores also maintained a second home in the Gainesboro Apartments in Nashville, where Livingfield was a member of the First Presbyterian Church, the Belle Meade Country Club, and the Hermitage Club. After Livingfield died February 9, 1934, at age sixty-six, Ellen and Livy returned to Nashville, where she built a house on land her father gave her on Lombardy Drive near his home. Edwin Keeble was the architect.[13]

Back home, the young widow met William Hatch "Will" Wemyss, a successful businessman. When their relationship became serious, Ellen told Will that she had a lifetime interest in a trust her deceased husband had established but that her interest would terminate should she remarry. Will solved the problem by giving Ellen an amount equal to the present value of the trust income she would have received had she remained single.[14] By this time, Ellen had learned a lot about Will. She knew that, in 1895, the year she was born, he graduated from a military academy and, the same year, at age sixteen, went to Louisville to work for Witherspoon Brothers Shoe Company. She also learned that, in 1902, her future husband and another Tennessean employed by the Witherspoon firm, James Franklin Jarman, returned to Nashville to take jobs with Carter Shoe Company. Will and Jarman founded Jarman Shoe Company in Nashville in 1924. That firm became General Shoe in 1933, and, later, Genesco. Jarman was president and CEO and Will was executive vice president from the company's founding until Will's retirement in 1949.[15]

In 1934, Will bought the historic Fairvue plantation in Sumner County, not far south of Gallatin on U.S. Highway 31-E. That same year, his wife, the former Helen Peters of St. Charles, Louisiana, died, leaving him to rear their son and daughter, William H. Wemyss Jr. and Peggy Wemyss. When Will and Ellen married in 1939, Will was in the midst of restoring Fairvue, built by Isaac Franklin in 1832. It took him eight months to complete the project and once more make Fairvue not only beautiful but also structurally sound.[16]

Once she was living in Sumner County, where her husband raised tobacco and had an impressive herd of cattle, Ellen became active in church and historic preservation efforts there while continuing to maintain her friends and activities in Davidson County. For the next forty years, she would come to Nashville regularly to see her friends or attend meetings of the Garden Club of Nashville, the Review Club, and the Study Club. She also was a Colonial Dame and was corresponding secretary of the Old Woman's Home on West End Avenue. Ellen was also a charter member of the Junior League of Nashville,[17] and a stalwart member of the Ladies' Hermitage Association, where she would become an icon. For decades, she would enjoy having friends from Nashville come to Fairvue for tea, beaten biscuits, homemade orange marmalade, fresh strawberries dipped in confectioner's sugar, and Scotch shortbread made with real butter.[18]

In Sumner County, Ellen was a member of the Friends of Cragfont in Castalian Springs. In 1958, she and Will were instrumental in influencing the State of Tennessee to purchase the historic site. Ellen was then put in charge of its restoration.[19] She was a lifetime member of the Bledsoe's Lick Historical Association, and took great pride in being cofounder with Will of The Church of Our Saviour, Episcopal, in Gallatin.[20]

Ellen's friends in Nashville and Sumner County grew to love her for her dedication to preservation, her loyalty to her friends, and ready approachability by anyone, without regard for their rank or station. These were key strong points in the makeup of her character.

Ellen must have felt snake-bitten when she learned from the U.S. Army Corps of Engineers in the 1950s that she and Will would lose approximately half of their seven hundred-acre farm when the Old Hickory Dam on the Cumberland River became a reality.[21] The dam materialized in 1957, and the family lost three hundred twenty-eight of their seven hundred acres to the ninety-mile long lake. Determined to make the best of the situation, Ellen and Will built a boat dock, and had a boat. In November of that year, Ellen told a reporter for *The Nashville Tennessean*, "I go boating and fishing, but I've decided water skiing is not for me. I tried it last summer. I ached for two weeks."[22]

In 1964, when the Ladies' Hermitage Association acquired Tulip Grove, Ellen was named "chairman of the restoration committee."[23] Her preservation efforts were rewarded four years later when Zone VI of the Garden Club of America gave her its Conservation Award for "her inspirational guidance in the acquisition and restoration of Tulip Grove and Cragfont."[24] The Garden Club of America followed suit in 1970 when, at its fifty-seventh annual meeting in Boston, the national president, Mrs. Jerome K. Doolan, presented Ellen with the Amy Angell Collier Montague Medal for her work in historical preservation. She was cited for having been a member of the board of the Ladies' Hermitage Association since 1949 and regent from 1951–1955. "Mrs. Wemyss," the president said, "was a guiding force in restoring the Hermitage to its former grandeur and elegance."

Ellen's husband of thirty-three years, William H. "Will" Wemyss, died at Fairvue on March 19, 1973, at age ninety-three. He had been ill for several months. After his retirement from Genesco, he remained a member of its board of governors until his death. He also was on the board of Third National Bank, a position he had held since 1939. In addition to Ellen, he was survived by his son and daughter, as well as ten grandchildren.[25]

Left a widow living alone in a large mansion, Ellen, at age seventy-eight, was vulnerable but didn't think so. Her son Livy was a serious farmer on his own property, River Grange, outside Franklin, Tennessee, and her stepchildren led busy lives in Nashville. She laughed, "Everybody thought I'd move back to Nashville after Will died, but I love it out here. It keeps me busy. I have this place to look after and the restored slave quarters to rent. I still sell tobacco and cattle."[26] Ellen never gave a thought to moving back to Nashville. She carried on as before, enjoyed her life at Fairvue, and got along quite well with two house servants and a good farm manager.

In 1980, when she was eighty-five, Ellen's speedboat caught fire on Old Hickory Lake. This happened shortly after the boat was refueled at the marina on East Camp Creek. After the rest of the party abandoned the boat, Ellen unsuccessfully tried to extinguish the fire. When that didn't work, she threw her dog overboard and swam to shore.[27]

Ellen was rewarded for all her hard work at Fairvue. In 1979, The U.S. Department of the Interior designated her home a national historic landmark. The unveiling of the plaque took place at a garden party hosted by Ellen on the afternoon of June 1.[28] In 1982, she was named Citizen of the Year in Sumner County and in 1989, Supporter of the Year of Greater Gallatin Inc.[29]

The Gallatin Police Department was protective of Ellen, who was beginning to drive a little erratically. Consequently, whenever her car was spotted on Gallatin city streets, the police would keep tabs by following her. Once when Ellen's good friend Walter Durham was having his car serviced in a Gallatin service station, he could not help but listen to the police radio that happened to be on. Here's what he heard: "Mrs. Wemyss has just pulled off the Nashville Highway on St. Blaise Road."[30]

———◦◦◦◦———

Bill Coke will always remember a cold, snowy weekend shortly after New Year's Day in the late 1970s, when most of the parents and children on South Stanford Drive and South Stanford Court were sledding. Ellen happened to spend that weekend with her brother and sister-in-law, Walter and Ophelia Stokes, who lived on the top of Stanford Drive. That cold afternoon, Ellen walked down from the Stokes's house, arriving at the top of South Stanford Court just as Bill Coke walked up the hill pulling his sled. Here is what Bill remembers: "We had been chatting for a minute or two, when I said, 'Mrs. Wemyss, would you like to go down on the sled?' Mrs. Wemyss replied, 'I believe I will.' Before I could protest, she had given me her keys and some letters she was holding, and laid down on the sled and was off. I frantically raced after her, feeling sure that she would fall off and hurt herself. I needn't have worried. She had a fast and successful run and, when she got off the sled and I had returned her keys and her mail to her, she said, 'That was fun!'"[31]

———◦◦◦◦———

In October 1982, when Ellen was eighty-seven, she still had the stamina to ride horseback with her son for more than two hours over his place in Williamson County without becoming fatigued.[32]

Ellen Wemyss, wearing a straw hat, at the Ladies Hermitage Association picnic. Photo courtesy of the Nashville Public Library, Special Collections.

Fairvue, long recognized as one of the showplaces of Middle Tennessee, was the scene of a movie star happening in 1982 or 1983 when Metro-Goldwyn-Mayer threw a *Gone With The Wind* anniversary party at the plantation house. The party was attended by Mary Astor, Eleanor Parker, and Janet Leigh, among others.[33]

At the spring outing of the Ladies' Hermitage Association in 1983, Fletch Coke, a future regent, had the pleasure of introducing Ellen as the guest speaker. Fletch simply said, "I never before had the pleasure of introducing an eighty-eight-year-old lady who had received three speeding tickets in the past year."[34] The audience loved it.

With some regularity in the 1980s and 1990s, Ellen and Walter Durham and his wife, Anna, would be going to the same affair in Nashville. Invariably, the Durhams would go by Fairvue and pick up Ellen. On one such occasion, they went together to a wedding at The Downtown Presbyterian Church. When the music was playing before the scheduled start of the wedding, Ellen began to tell Anna and Walter, in a low voice, stories of other marriage ceremonies that, for one reason or another, were late starting or didn't take place at all. As the minutes passed, Ellen continued her stories, complete with names and details, but in a louder voice. Up until the time the wedding finally started, all the people seated nearby were listening with fascination as Ellen continued her interesting tales.

One time, when Ellen rode with the Durhams to a party that she knew would last until late in the evening, she shouted back to her cook, Margaret Malone, who was nearly as old as Ellen, "Go on to bed. I'll be home late."

When Anna and Walter's youngest daughter, Anna Durham Windrow, was a teenager, she and several Gallatin friends boarded their horses at Fairvue. Mrs. Durham would often take them there and pick them up after their ride. Once, when Ellen was in her eighties, she invited Mrs. Durham to bring her swimming suit and go swimming in Old Hickory Lake. Anna did so and the two ladies walked down to the water's edge in their bathing suits and enjoyed swimming together.[35]

Sometimes it didn't suit Ellen to ride with the Durhams. One such night, they and Ellen left a Gallatin social affair late in the evening. Anna insisted that Walter drive Ellen's car to Fairvue and that she would follow in their car. Ellen would not allow Walter to drive but did consent for him to ride with her in the front seat. They had not gone far at all before Ellen drove on the median strip of a Gallatin street and generally scared Walter to death before she managed to get home.[36]

Once, late in life, a policeman stopped Mrs. Wemyss for driving too slow. She said to him, "You people have got to make up your minds. The last time I got a ticket, it was for driving too fast."

Nashville's Query Club celebrated its one-hundredth birthday on October 1, 1985. Naturally, Ellen was there, as her mother had been one of the founders of the club in 1885. With her to celebrate the event at Cheekwood's Pineapple Room were such good friends as Henriette Weaver Jackson, Sara Rodes, Mary Parrent, Margaret Lindsley Warden, Mildred Stoves, and Rowena Ferguson. The women's literary club, the oldest in the city, appropriately had as its topic for 1985, "The 1880s."[37]

Ellen continued to ride her horse occasionally until, at age ninety-two, her son worried so much about her falling that she gave it up.[38] Ellen continued to drive, however, until she was ninety-seven. Despite the fact that her Gallatin friends kept an eye out for her on the road as she was somewhat erratic and paid little heed to speed limits, it should be said that she had no history of having any serious automobile wrecks.

The last preservation award presented to Ellen Wemyss came in 1993 when she was among fourteen Tennessee residents chosen statewide for the Tennessee Historical Commission's award for historic preservation. The awards were announced during Historic Preservation Week. Ellen had been nominated for the honor by another long-time friend, Hortense Cooper, wife of the late former Governor Prentice Cooper and mother of U.S. Representative Jim Cooper.

Ellen's son, Livy, his wife Agnes Fort More, and their daughter Ellen, who was named for her grandmother, gave an elegant party at the Belle Meade Country Club to celebrate Ellen's one-hundredth birthday. Ellen was, that evening, riding in a wheelchair, elaborately decorated by Aggie More and pushed by Sam Henderson, another legendary Nashville character. The evening was a celebration of a life well lived and a time for reminiscences. "Granny Happy" said, "I used to be 5'3" but I've shrunk three inches."[39] She spoke of growing up on Hillsboro Pike, recalling, "My father rode horseback to town for fifteen years, until automobiles ran him off the road, and my mother drove a horse and buggy to downtown Nashville to shop." She also said how fortunate she was to be able to still live at Fairvue and expressed appreciation for her family; for her long-time cooks, Margaret Malone and Ruth Holder; and her capable and loyal farm manager, Corbitt Clark, who had, she said, "served as the farm's overseer for the past thirty years." Someone that evening made the point that Ellen, who was known for her warmth and charm, resembled Fairvue's first mistress, Adelicia Hayes Acklen, in many ways. Adelicia arrived at Fairvue in 1839 and Ellen arrived one hundred years later, in 1939. Both women were active horse-women, gracious hostesses, and daughters of prominent Nashville attorneys. At the celebration, Ellen attributed her long life to "keeping busy and keeping interested in things." One friend

Ellen Wemyss sitting in her parlor at Fairvue in 1995. Photo courtesy of the Nashville Public Library, Special Collections.

remarked, "She's quite a gal and thoroughly modern. I remember she was the first woman to wear pants to the Ladies' Hermitage Association meeting in the days when it wasn't done."[40] Ann (Mrs. Charles) Wells, who served on the Hermitage board with "Miss Ellen" in the 1980s, and was at Ellen's one-hundredth birthday party, thought of her as a dear friend, who was a determined and relentless advocate for her ideas, but also someone willing to listen to the other side.[41] What a wonderful evening, for a wonderful lady.

Ellen's subsequent birthday was more subdued. She celebrated it with her family and friends. A friend and admirer said, "She enjoys her historic home in Gallatin, eating turnip greens, and reminiscing about the significant social and historical changes she has seen." Among her birthday gifts were one hundred and one roses.[42]

When she was well past the centennial mark, Ellen went to see the movie *Titanic* when it was all the rage. Of the millions who saw the film, she was one of the few who could remember when the ship sank in 1912.[43]

At age one hundred and two, Ellen attended the opening of the Wildhorse Saloon on Nashville's historic Second Avenue. Later that same year, shortly before Ellen's next birthday, a family member said, "Happy will be one hundred and three years old. She is healthy, her memory is sharp, and she exudes contentment and vitality. You have got to change. That is what life is all about."[44]

Ellen Stokes More Wemyss died at Fairvue on June 4, 2001, at age one hundred and six.[45] She had lived to see three centuries, a remarkable feat, and had been, for decades, one of the Nashville area's most prominent citizens. She may have been the state's oldest registered voter. Called "Miss Ellen" by so many of her friends, Ellen kept up the fight for historic preservation to the very end. In recent years, she had spearheaded the effort to save Rosemont, the historic home in Gallatin that, in the nineteenth century, had been the home of Josephus Conn Guild, author of *Old Times In Tennessee.* Miss Ellen put up $50,000 and inspired other preservationists to match that amount. Her last preservation fight came when she was ninety-nine. That time, she joined an unsuccessful lawsuit to keep Walmart from building a big box store on Highway 31-E, a road lined with pastures, barns, and grand plantation homes, including Fairvue, which Ellen and Will Wemyss had so lovingly restored and maintained.[46]

Chapter 13

Margaret Early Wyatt
1903–2001

M argaret Wyatt was a first cousin of my wife Irene's father, Granbery Jackson Jr. As such, we saw quite a lot of her. She was an Unreconstructed Rebel to the core. Visiting her at a nursing home later in life, she told my wife and me loudly that we had to get her out of there. The others were not like her—the Yankees among them being the most offensive.[1]

———◦◦◦———

Born thirty-eight years after the end of the Civil War, Margaret Evans Early Wyatt was the granddaughter of John Fletcher Early, a Confederate soldier in the Army of Tennessee. She grew up hearing stories of the heroism of Southern soldiers and the righteousness of their cause. So strong was her devotion that she never liked to use the word "north" at all. After she moved to Wyatt Hall in 1946, one mile north of Franklin on Franklin Pike, she referred to her antebellum home as being seventeen miles south of Nashville rather than one mile north of Franklin.

Margaret was the oldest of five children born to John and Willie Evans Fall Early. She was born August 17, 1903, at her parents' home, Pontotoc, three and one-half miles from the Nashville Public

Square on the corner of Greenwood and Scott avenues in East Nashville. Her brother, John Early Jr., was born April 8, 1905, at the home of their maternal grandparents, Mr. and Mrs. Joseph Horton Fall, at 303 North Vine Street. Her sister, Katherine "Kay" Wyche Early, was born August 18, 1909, at Pontotoc, as were a younger brother and sister, Joseph Horton Fall Early on January 14, 1913, and Elizabeth Drennon "Lib" Early on March 6, 1916. When Margaret was very small, Pontotoc, formerly a summer home, had a furnace, a big black iron coal range, coal grate fireplaces in every room, running water, and four bedrooms. Their bathroom was a three-hole outhouse in the back yard. There was also an engine house, a big barn, and a shed where the cows were milked. There were other buildings for carriages and buggies and other horse stalls. Mrs. Early also had an orchard, a grape arbor, and flower and vegetable gardens. There were also cornfields, a big pasture, and forest trees. In the front yard were two small summer houses, one on each side. All in all, Pontotoc was an idyllic place in which to grow up.

Mr. Early had many stallions and other horses. His best horse was The Emperor, who held the American pacing record of 2:09 3/4 at the turn of the century. Mr. Early owned Early-Cain Company at 315 North Market Street. The building had three floors and a freight elevator. It was the finest harness store in Nashville, and manufactured and sold harnesses, saddles, and horse goods. He rode to town each day in a buggy pulled by The Emperor, keeping it, during the day, at a livery stable on Front Street. Margaret first went to Ross School. One day, in 1916, her teacher told the children to put on their coats and go straight home. Margaret bicycled home as fast as she could, realizing quickly that there was a big fire as the wind was blowing smoke and burned wood directly into her eyes. Pontotoc was spared but much of East Nashville was destroyed by the biggest fire in Nashville history.

Even as a small child, Margaret loved hanging around the barn with its distinctive smells and activity. Every morning, as soon as she got dressed, Margaret would run down to the stable to see what had happened overnight. When she was small, her father gave her a Shetland pony named Lady Enon. When the pony died, Mr. Early gave her one named Dinkey, which had been owned by Vanderbilt University Chancellor James Kirkland's daughter. Margaret was still so little she had to be helped on its back, where she sat on a pad held in place by a girth. Margaret's next pony, Dorothy, was her very own, given her by her Grandfather Fall. Margaret, who loved animals as much as she hated school, had been taught how to plait Dorothy's mane. But the pony that Margaret had the longest and loved the most was named Little Britches. He was spotted white and chestnut and was very headstrong. By then, Margaret was old enough to have a riding habit with boots that laced up. She also had the proficiency and her father's permission to ride almost anywhere, including over the Woodland Street Bridge to his store in town.

Margaret's eleventh year was exciting. Her grandfather J. H. "Papa" Fall took her with him and his second wife to New York City (Margaret's grandmother, Margaret Evans Fall, for whom she was named, died in 1911). The aspect of the trip Margaret most treasured was her visit to Tiffany & Co., where Papa bought her a beautiful coral necklace. The other milestone was not as exciting but more lasting. After age eleven, Margaret never cut her hair. For the rest of her long life, she wore her hair in a bun.

One of the delights of Margaret's childhood was to go to the races at the State Fairgrounds, where her father was the starter for the races from 1903 until his death in 1934. The Tennessee State Fair opened the second week in September, one week after classes started at Peabody Demonstration School, where Margaret was then a student. Each year, Margaret begged her father to write a note to excuse her from school in time for her to ride the streetcar from Peabody to the Public Square and walk down the hill to the livery stable, where she and her father would ride to the races for five successive days. Mr. Early did write the note, and at the races, Margaret would sit under the judges' stand to watch. Soon, she knew all the grooms, trainers, and drivers. Years later, when the race track was torn up for auto races, Margaret's reaction was, "It's awful."

When Margaret was a teenager, she and her first cousin, John Early Jackson, shared an interest in séances. Whenever Margaret spent a weekend with the Jacksons, which was often, she and John Early would rub their hands together to create some "electricity" and then put them on a tabletop and ask the spirits to thump the table or make it walk. "It was really scary," she later recalled. Aunt Margaret, John Early's mother, would invariably make them stop.

One summer at the Monteagle Sunday School Assembly, Margaret's father introduced her to Dr. Bruce R. Payne, president of George Peabody College. While the three of them were sitting on a log, a lizard joined them. Margaret picked up a stone and threw it at the lizard, cutting its tail off. Dr. Payne jokingly told Margaret, "Tonight, you're going to hear a scratching at your bedroom door and its going to be that lizard saying, 'I want my tailypo.'" Margaret said, "Oh, I don't believe in stuff like that." From then on, Dr. Payne and Margaret called each other "Tailypo."

One day after recess, Margaret went up to Dr. Payne's office and asked to see him. Dr. Payne was pleased to see her. Margaret got right to the point, telling him how much she hated algebra and that she didn't want to take it any longer. He told Margaret she ought to take it. "But, I don't want to," she said. "It makes me sick just to think about it. I don't want to ever go to college." So, finally, Dr. Payne said, "All right." Margaret was "thrilled to death," so pleased that a few weeks later she went back to his office and said, "Now, Tailypo, as you know I don't want to go to college, and I want to stop taking this Latin—amo, amas, amat—I can't stand it!" He said, "I really think you ought to take Latin, as it helps you understand the English language so much better." Margaret said, "I already understand the English language!" He finally gave up, saying, "All right." Margaret said, "Thank you soooo much!" She had stayed in his office so long she was late for her next class. So she ran to the psychology building and jerked open the door, only to confront Dr. Thomas Alexander, the stern principal of the school. He was furious when he found out that Margaret had gone over his head to Dr. Payne and had received permission to drop both algebra and Latin. Margaret figured she was the only student at Peabody Demonstration School to graduate without passing algebra or Latin. It really didn't matter what Dr. Alexander thought.

After graduation, Margaret taught riding at Camp Riva-Lake for two summers and for one summer at Camp Cohechee, a girls' camp that Ward-Belmont ran in Fryeburg, Maine. The only contact Margaret had with New Englanders that summer, other than the locals in camp, were the blacksmiths who shod her horses. They couldn't understand her Southern accent and were, according to her, impolite. Just as bad, she couldn't understand them. Margaret said, "Deliver me from these damn Yankees."

Margaret also taught riding at Ward-Belmont from 1924 until 1927, and put on a horse show there each spring. On the side, she showed horses. Each summer, she went with her paternal aunt Margaret Early Jackson and her husband Granbery Jackson (who taught in the Vanderbilt School of Engineering) to their Tindall Farm near Zion Presbyterian Church in Maury County. She rode with them and their sons, her first cousins, John Early and Granbery, in Mr. Jackson's big blue Cadillac touring car. Whenever they were together, Mrs. Jackson always reminded Margaret that she wanted her to marry at the Jacksons' home.

In the fall of 1923, Metro Film Studio, forerunner of Metro-Goldwyn-Mayer, sent director Allen Holubar and a supporting cast to Williamson County to recreate the Battle of Franklin for a movie to be known as *The Human Mill*. Although the movie was never made, Margaret enthusiastically participated. "My part," she later said, "was to run out on the upstairs veranda (at the Cheairs Mansion in Spring Hill) and unfurl the Confederate flag." Unfurling Confederate flags was something Margaret did all her life.

Hubert Wyatt saw Margaret Early for the first time when she was walking down the aisle at the Princess Theater. Characteristically, she had on a big hat. Hubert asked Margaret's date, whom he knew, for an introduction. The young man introduced them and soon after, Hubert asked her for a date. Margaret learned that Hubert was a traveling salesman for Neely-Harwell and Company, a Nashville dry goods house; that his territory was West Kentucky, where he grew up; that he was two years older than she was, and was the youngest salesman the company had; and that he was unusually out-going and self-confident. He normally came to Nashville on weekends, where he had a rented room. Consequently, Hubert and Margaret usually dated on Saturday nights.

Margaret and Hubert became engaged on Christmas night, 1926. When she told her parents of her engagement, Margaret, half-jokingly, announced she wanted to get married on horseback at the Horse Show Pavilion at the Tennessee State Fairgrounds with Tony Rose providing the music. "Then," she said, "I could invite all my friends, both white and colored." Mrs. Early put a stop to that so Margaret got married the day Ward-Belmont was out, June 2, 1927, at her Aunt Margaret Jackson's new house, Graystone, on Franklin

Pike. A beautiful rehearsal party was held at Pontotoc. For her wedding, Margaret wore her Grandmother Fall's wedding dress and her gorgeous antique jewelry.

<hr />

Until she married Hubert, Margaret had never tasted alcohol, due to her strict Methodist upbringing. She had been brought up in Hobson Chapel Methodist Church only a short distance down Greenwood Avenue from Pontotoc. Her only connection with illicit whiskey had been when, as a child visiting the Monteagle Sunday School Assembly, Mr. Edward Craig showed her and four or five other children some moonshiners that he had assembled on the train to take to Nashville. Margaret remembered they were handcuffed and had black whiskers and wore old clothes and black hats.

Once, not long after she married, Margaret and her mother had the flu. Hubert brought them some whiskey, saying, "What you need is a good hot toddy." Just then, Mr. Early came in the bedroom and said to Margaret, "Don't drink that." Margaret said, "Father, I have always tried to please you, and now I am married to Hubert, so I'm going to do what he asks me to do." Mr. Early walked out of the room and never ever said another word about Margaret not drinking. She took a swig or two and said, "I now know the shape of my esophagus!" Mrs. Early was reluctant. She told Hubert, "I'm afraid to drink this, Hubert. This whiskey might be 'jake leg,' so I'm not going to drink it." Margaret recovered from the flu the next day. Mrs. Early was in bed for days. Hubert felt vindicated.

<hr />

On the Sunday before the 1933 Tennessee State Fair opened, Hubert and Margaret drove to Nashville from Gallatin, where they were then living, to see who brought harness horses to race. They saw their friend, Dr. Hugh Parshall of Urbana, Ohio, a wonderful vet, trainer, and driver, who was setting up his big stable. The Wyatts invited Dr. Parshall to spend the night with them, promising to get him back to his stable early the next day. He accepted. The

Margaret Wyatt riding J. E. Vonian to a world record at the
Tennessee State Fairgrounds on September 11, 1933.
Photo courtesy of Kay Russell (Mrs. Earl) Beasley.

next morning, after letting Hubert off in Nashville so he could catch a train to New York, Dr. Parshall asked Margaret if she would like to drive in a race. Margaret, who always had her riding habit and boots in the trunk of her car, said, "I certainly would." When Margaret asked, "When?" Dr. Parshall said, "Today," and told her she would be riding J. E. Vonian. He instructed her to be back at 10:30 AM to warm up the horse. Excited to death, Margaret drove to her parents' new home on Belmont Boulevard, Wychewood, and told her mother that, if she ever wanted to see her daughter race, she had to come to the fairgrounds that afternoon. Then she called her father at his office and told him the same thing. Next, she called Hubert and told him what she was about to do. He postponed his trip to New York, and he and Mr. and Mrs. Early were there to see Margaret line her sulky up with three other pacers for the second event of the afternoon, a three-heat $200 purse event. Margaret knew that the Tennessee State Fairgrounds track was considered the second best in the country, only behind The Red Mile in Lexington, Kentucky. Margaret also knew from her practice run that J. E. Vonian was both fast and powerful. As the race started, Margaret thought to herself, "This can't be real." Despite sitting on a sulky seat that had to be modified to fit her slight form, and being the only woman in the race, Margaret won all three heats. As she was getting out of her sulky, she saw reporters running toward her shouting, "You and J .E. Vonian just set a world's record." Indeed, she did for lady drivers in a competitive race. Her times were 2:04 3/4; 2:04 1/4; and 2:05. She won again with J. E. Vonian four days later, on September 15, 1933.

Margaret became pregnant when she and Hubert were living in Shelbyville, Tennessee, in 1934. Her only baby, a perfectly formed little boy, was stillborn at the Bedford County Hospital. The umbilical cord had wrapped around his neck and choked him to death. Margaret and Hubert were devastated. The baby's death, nevertheless, tightened the bond between Margaret and her niece, Kay Early Russell Beasley, born two months earlier. Later, Kay and her little sister, Ellen Fall Russell Sadler, would visit the Wyatts in Charlotte, North Carolina, and Elkton, Kentucky. Their first cousin, Margaret Frierson Early Ross, named for Margaret Wyatt, also made the visit to Elkton. Having Kay and Ellen out of the house was helpful as their mother, Kay Early Russell, gave birth to a third daughter, Elizabeth Lee Russell Brown, that summer.

One day in the early 1930s, when the Wyatts were living in Nashville, Hubert came home and announced to Margaret, "I have something important to tell you, and you must not mention it to a soul." Margaret could see that Hubert was worried about this, and just before he started to tell her what was on his mind, she said, "Wait a minute, I'll tell you." So Margaret told Hubert exactly what he intended to tell her, even naming the people involved. Hubert interrupted her to say, "How do you know this? A man told me just awhile ago." Margaret said, "I don't know, unless it's mental telepathy. I'm reading your mind, I guess." Then, Hubert said, "You are a witch."

Margaret's mental telepathy would continue to manifest itself. In the summer of 1936, Hubert, while traveling with Margaret in Texas, got a call from Montgomery Ward & Co. asking him to come to New York as soon as possible. Hubert returned to Nashville, dropped off Margaret, and took a train to New York. This gave Margaret an opportunity to visit friends in Woodbury, Tennessee. The next night, Margaret woke up with a premonition that she and Hubert were moving to New York City. When he called to tell her of the job offer the next morning, Margaret already knew about it. Hubert accepted the position. His new responsibility would be to buy all the work clothes for Montgomery Ward's stores. Hubert and Margaret drove to New York where she found the perfect, furnished apartment at 120 East Sixty-fifth Street. Included in some horse pictures on a wall was one of Alligator, a steeplechase horse owned by Mrs. M. K. Stevenson of Roslyn, New York. Margaret couldn't believe her eyes as she and Hubert had witnessed Alligator win the Southern Grasslands Hunt and Racing Foundation International Steeplechase on December 6, 1930, at Gallatin, Tennessee. Five months after moving to New York, Hubert and Margaret decided they didn't want to live there. He resigned and they moved back to Nashville. As Hubert was about to enter the Holland Tunnel, he turned to Margaret and said, "Don't you want to look back at your old hometown?" Margaret quipped, "If I never see it again, it suits me." Their next move was to Charlotte, North Carolina, where Hubert was responsible for selling Red Kap work clothing to Belk stores from Florida to Washington, D.C. They enjoyed living in North Carolina and spent their leisure time owning birddogs and harness horses, hunting quail, attending harness races across the country, and talking about horses.

With World War II came gas rationing. This meant that there was no way Hubert could call on his customers across coastal Georgia, the Carolinas, and Virginia. Hubert and Margaret came back to Middle Tennessee where Hubert first managed Red Kap's

Dickson plant, which was challenged by having lost so many men to military service. The Wyatts next moved to Clarksville, a town overrun with soldiers. Hubert worked hard to improve efficiency at the Red Kap plant there. Nearby was a large Goodrich plant that had been converted into making gas masks. The company desperately needed carriers for the gas masks. Still working for Red Kap, Hubert knew about this, and Red Kap bought a grocery store on the town square in Elkton, Kentucky. Hubert converted it into a factory making gas mask carriers. Eventually, he had shifts of women working around the clock. His office was in a gas station. He and Margaret bought a house in Elkton. He put up a dog kennel and Margaret put in a vegetable garden. She was also head of the Todd County Red Cross chapter.

While living in Elkton, Hubert bought a fine bird dog named Blue Willing Jean. He bred her to the National Field Trial Champion. Unfortunately, the cute puppies died of distemper. Margaret said, "It was awful." Blue Willing Jean was bred again to a fine hound and this time, the Wyatts kept one of the pups that they named Cud'n Nick for one of Hubert's ancestors, Nicholas Wyatt. Nick turned out to be a fighter and particularly liked to fight another of the Wyatts' dogs. Hubert had to work to keep them apart.

<hr>

On June 2, 1946, Hubert and Margaret bought their early Federal house on Franklin Pike not far from Franklin. They had admired the house since they first married, but then did not have the means to buy it even if it had been on the market. The house that they named Wyatt Hall was Hubert's anniversary gift to Margaret. It faced south between the highway and the L&N Railroad tracks that ran extremely close to the kitchen, which was actually on the railroad right-of-way. The house had been built about 1815.

The spring after moving to Wyatt Hall, Margaret was sitting in the front yard looking at a huge wild cherry tree and thinking, "I don't know what that big scar is on its bark." Suddenly, the scar started moving up the tree. Margaret instinctively yelled, "Snake, snake!" to Hubert, who was in the house. He came to the front door and said, "Where?" Margaret said, "On the cherry tree." Hubert got his gun and

Wyatt Hall located in Franklin, Tennessee was the home of Mr. and Mrs. W. Hubert Wyatt. Photo courtesy of Arthur R. Ezell.

shot the snake that Margaret insisted was as big as her arm. Hubert assured her that, although big, the chicken snake was harmless. Margaret said, "Don't kid me. I don't go for that harmless stuff." Later, they found the snake's mate up close to the house. Hubert also killed it. When Margaret was all alone, she went upstairs and was just about to get in the tub when she looked out the window at the same cherry tree and saw another huge snake climbing up the tree trunk. Having been taught by Hubert how to put a shell in his gun and squint down the sight and pull the trigger, Margaret, who was barefooted and in her birthday suit, slipped on a dress, ran downstairs, grabbed the gun, put a shell in it, flew out the front door, and shot the snake in the head. Realizing that she was barefooted and upset that the snake was "taking on so," she ran back in the house and locked the screen door and watched. After a few minutes, she decided to take her bath, taking time out every now and then to look out the window. The snake was still there. She then went downstairs and cooked dinner, interrupted by glances at the tree to make sure it hadn't crawled off. When Hubert finally pulled in off Franklin Pike, she ran to the gate, shouting "I'm Annie Oakley." On a later occasion, while talking on the telephone, Margaret spotted a snake's head on her mantel. She yelled, "Snake on the mantel!" slammed down the phone and hollered to Uncle Jim Bailey, a black man who worked for Hubert, "Snake, snake!" He came running in and said, "Now, Miss Margaret, you didn't see no snake in here." Knowing that her eyes did not lie, Margaret told Jim to get the stepladder. She got up on it and saw that the mantel was about one and a half inches away from the wall. She then told Uncle Jim to bring her a butcher knife and some steel wool that she packed into the gap.

Margaret had to go to town a little later. When she returned, the first thing she did was look at that mantel. Sure enough, the snake was back. So, she yelled to Jim, "Snake, snake!" As he ran by the woodpile to the house, he grabbed a stick of wood that he used to kill the snake. All Uncle Jim could say was, "I shore wouldn't have believed it if I hadn't seen it." Margaret once again climbed up on the stepladder to see how in the world that snake got in. Convinced that there was another snake in her bedroom, Margaret took her cat and a bird dog to her bedroom to see if they could see any movement that she could not. "It was awful." A little later, Hubert called to say he wanted her to go to Knoxville that night and to pack her bag. Margaret said, "I'm dee-lighted to go." As soon as they got to the motel where they were staying, Margaret looked under the bed and under the chairs for snakes. "I was a wreck," she said. On the way home the next day, she told Hubert, "This is the first time in my life that I ever hated to go home." Hubert tried to kid her, but Margaret told him pretty quickly, "I am in no mood for frivolous talk." The next day, when dressing for a luncheon in Franklin, Margaret noticed little red bumps around her waist and lower back. Thinking, "I'll put some rubbing alcohol on it," she did so and burst into tears because it burned so. She said, "It's killing me." When her doctor told her she had shingles, Margaret was convinced that it was brought on "by this snake stuff."

One year, a saddle horse friend from West Kentucky brought the Wyatts six game chickens: two cocks and four hens. Pretty soon, the two cocks got into a bloody fight to determine which one would be boss. They nearly killed each other. In time, a Nashville gambler who said his name was Blackie showed up at Wyatt Hall, hoping to buy "Boss Man." Margaret looked at the man, sizing him up. Then, she asked, "Is that your alias?" The Wyatts ended up selling Blackie four or five cocks. Pretty soon, Blackie, whose real name was George Orville Mayfield, had his chicken-fighting arena in Nashville raided even though he had paid off the police. The affair ended up with the chickens being confiscated and taken to jail in their cages. About 2 AM the next morning, the police called the owners telling them to come get the cocks because no one in the jail could get any sleep for their crowing. *The Nashville Tennessean* carried the story, which Margaret's mother read. Suspicious that some of Margaret and Hubert's cocks were involved, she called Margaret to ask if she knew Mr. Mayfield. Margaret said, "I certainly do. He's one of my friends. He's out here right now putting a shingle roof on the smokehouse." Sometime later, Blackie showed up at Wyatt Hall in what Margaret described as "an old black, rattletrap car." He told Hubert he was down on his luck and wanted to buy some cocks on credit. The Wyatts, disenchanted with the gamecock business, told him to help himself to all the cocks he wanted and that they would eat the rest. Everyone was happy.

Somewhere along the line, a friend in Florida called to say he wanted to give the Wyatts the pick of the litter from the mating of a Weimaraner bitch and a male dog the friend owned. Hubert thanked the man and said, "No thanks. I already have a kennel full of bird dogs and puppies coming along, to boot." Margaret had other ideas and said, "Give the dog to me." After putting down the phone, Hubert, a little upset, said, "Margaret, what in hell did you say that for?" Margaret replied, "He will be interesting to have around here as there are no Weimaraners around here." When the beautiful

Weimaraner arrived, Margaret named him Jubal for Lieutenant General Jubal A. Early, C.S.A., a distant kinsman. One day, Margaret hung a pair of nylon stockings on a clothesline on the back porch. Later, when she went to get them, only one was there. Suspecting that Jubal had swallowed the stocking, Margaret and "our colored man, Norvell," took Jubal out in the yard. Norvell held him while Margaret tried to pour mineral oil down his throat. She emptied the entire bottle. Margaret later told Hubert, "I think I got more on the outside of me than I had on the inside of him." Four or five hours later, Norvell brought Mrs. Wyatt the stocking on a stick. Margaret washed the stocking and wore it to a dinner party that evening at the Belle Meade Country Club. She said to her dinner partner, whom she knew well, "Tom, look at this stocking. See how much lighter it is than the other one? You'll never guess where it has been today." When told what happened, the guests at the table suggested to Margaret that she appear on the syndicated TV show, *What's My Line?* Margaret was extremely fond of Jubal, despite his propensity for swallowing Hubert's socks and her nylon stockings.

Her sister, Elizabeth "Lib" McGaw, a sculptress who studied under Puryear Mims, wanted to make a life-sized statue of Jubal. So, Margaret took the dog to Lib's studio in her home on Nashville's Brighton Road for several sittings. Later, a pleased Margaret told Lib, "You've got a 'barking likeness.'" When Jubal died, Margaret had him buried in the back yard at Wyatt Hall, wrapped in a Confederate flag. She put his collar on the statue Lib made and positioned it in the front hall so all her friends could see it. The statue was such a good likeness that one of the Wyatts' other bird dogs that had hated Jubal attacked the statue every time he saw it.

Because Margaret's first cousin Granbery Jackson Jr. didn't hunt, his son, Granbery Jackson III, knew that, if he wanted to hunt, Hubert Wyatt was the man to teach him. Hubert was delighted to do so, as he was an excellent shot and had a collection of fine shotguns. When Granbery III was twelve years old in August 1957, Uncle Hubert gave him a shotgun. Granbery's sister, Irene Jackson Wills (my wife), who is seven and one-half years older than her brother, remembers driving

Granbery and his gun out to Wyatt Hall that month for his first shooting lesson. When they arrived, Cousin Margaret was in the kitchen cooking breakfast on her ancient, black stove. She was wearing high heels, an apron, and had on some of the spectacular diamond jewelry that Hubert loved to give her. That was typical attire.

Margaret, incidentally, was an excellent cook who enjoyed cooking turnip greens with hog jowl and canning peach preserves. She was also skilled at needlepoint and stitched twelve dining room chair covers of favorite horses and dogs, the designs of which were made by her friend, Mrs. Margaret Parshall of Millbrook, New York. Margaret also enjoyed painting. Two of her oil paintings of horses' heads hung in the dining room.

In 1961, Hubert bought Margaret a bay gelding pacer named Edgewood Frisco. They kept him and several other horses they owned at Sanders Russell's stable in Stevenson, Alabama, a long drive from Nashville. One day, Margaret said to Hubert, "I wish we could keep them a little closer to home so we could see them every day and work with them." Pretty soon, Hubert said he was going to "scout around and see if I can't find some land near our house, and, when I do, I'll build you a racetrack, so you can see them every day." Margaret's reply was "Oh, Hubert, that will be a big undertaking." Hubert persisted and leased from Dr. Dunklin Bowman, their dentist in Nashville, one hundred and twenty-five acres on Spencer Creek Road. Hubert got a ten-year lease and an option to lease the property for another ten years. It was perfect, with a creek; an old antebellum farmhouse, owned in the nineteenth century by Dr. Andrew B. Ewing; shade trees; and a barn that Hubert renovated. He built a half-mile track and designed his own training stable. When construction began, Margaret, who felt that her grandest dream was coming true, insisted on riding the huge earthmover down to the construction site. The workers also enclosed the farm with white fences and built stallion paddocks, a blacksmith shop, and a big tool shed to house Margaret's riding mower. The last piece of the puzzle was to write the United States Trotting Association for their racing colors: green and white with a big yellow "W" in the middle.

Margaret then went to the Tennessee State Fairgrounds to look for the big bell that her father started harness races with from 1906 until 1934. Officials found the bell in a shed and gave it to her.

The first horses arrived from a stable in Lexington, Kentucky, on December 4, 1964. On December 10, John Early was the first horse to train on the Wyatt track. How excited Margaret and Hubert were. In their gorgeous stable they had a sign printed and hung. It read:

<blockquote>
Speak gently to our horses,
do not yell or swear at them.
They are gentlemen and ladies by
instinct and should be treated as such.
Our stable is our horses' home, and it is our
pleasure to make it a happy one.
</blockquote>

Mr. and Mrs. W. H. Wyatt

Margaret loved the trains, with their deafening noise, that ran so close to the house. She and Hubert even got the names and addresses of the engineers and sent them Christmas cards each year. Many times, when friends or kinfolk would ride the train to Franklin, Margaret and Uncle Jim would stand by the tracks and wave a Confederate flag as the train whistled by Wyatt Hall. As soon as the train passed, Margaret would jump in her yellow Cadillac and beat the train to the station to be on hand to welcome whomever came to see her. Once, Jennie Gant, her mother, Miss Lou, and three or four other ladies rode the L&N from Nashville to Franklin. All had been given a corsage. When they approached Wyatt Hall, they all were on the right side of the train, looking for Uncle Jim and Margaret and their Confederate flag. On another occasion, an engineer invited Hubert to ride in the engine down to Brentwood. Of course, Hubert accepted and had Margaret and her mother drive down there to pick him up. It was dark and Mrs. Early was frightened. Margaret stopped at a flat place and left her headlights on so the engineer would know where to stop. Hubert was grinning and blowing the whistle when the train stopped right beside the car.

All her adult life, Margaret wore big hats. One she particularly loved "was a big brown felt hat with a bunch of colorful butterflies on the front that trembled when I moved. Just beautiful, even if I do say so." Margaret also enjoyed wearing diamond pear-shaped earrings and a gold cuff with diamond horseshoes that Hubert gave her. He bought them from Harry Winston in New York City.

Wherever she traveled with Hubert, Margaret was always on the lookout for interesting horseshoes to bring home for her collection. She had many framed, such as one of a Lipizzaner horse from Vienna that someone sent her in 1966. She found a round, antique, gold leaf frame with roses in four places that looked nice. She got some red velvet for the background and twisted the white tail hairs from the horse around the gold braid. When finished, Margaret was pleased. "It was most fitting, I think. Just so pretty." Pretty soon, framed horseshoes, many from world-famous horses, were all over the house and, later, a miniature horse was installed on the hood of her Cadillac.

In the late 1960s or possibly during the following decade, Margaret Wyatt called my wife to tell her that she had named a filly "Charming Irene" in Irene's honor. Naturally, Irene was flattered and even more pleased when "Charming Irene" won or placed in a race or two. The bubble burst, however, when Margaret sold "Charming Irene." The new owner changed her name. Still, not every woman has had a horse named for her.

Jack Daniel was one of many trotters that Hubert and Margaret bought as a yearling. They liked his looks and breeding, but Margaret could not stand his original name, Federal Victory. She told Hubert, "I simply couldn't race a horse with that name." Hubert said, "We'll change his name." And they did, to Jack Daniel after Hubert called Winton Smith at Jack Daniel's to ask his permission. Winton was delighted and said he'd like to make a blanket for the horse. Hubert said, "Let's wait and see how he does." Jack Daniel turned out great. Margaret loved going across the highway to Wyatt Hall Farm to train him. Her only problem was getting in the sulky. When he was hooked up, Jack Daniel would "cow kick;" without care, he could hit someone and break a leg. Margaret said he wasn't mean, just anxious to get started. When warming up horses, Margaret, not surprisingly, always wore a Confederate cap. Once at a race at Goshen, New York, a center for harness races, Margaret and Hubert expected Jack Daniel to win. After leading most of the race, he hobbled a little bit in the backstretch and lost by a short margin. Hubert went over to the paddock to see what happened. When he came back, he said, "Guess what? He lost a shoe." Margaret said, "Right here before all these damn Yankees, coming home in true Southern fashion, barefooted." Margaret and Hubert's hosts, Margaret and Daryl Parshall, got a laugh out of it. They knew perfectly well why Margaret changed Federal Victory's name.

Margaret and Hubert's yardman often dug up Civil War-era minie balls and cannon balls in their yard at Wyatt Hall. Once, excited about finding a cannon ball, Hubert and Margaret found someone capable of defusing it. When the specialist arrived, he said his name was Sherman. Margaret, who was not fond of William Tecumseh Sherman, refused to let him do the work. The minie balls and cannon balls were displayed at Wyatt Hall, as were a stack of Confederate bills; a wrinkled military pass that Margaret's grandfather carried to pass from Nashville to Gallatin during the war; and the surgical chest that Dr. Watson Gentry used when he amputated the leg of Confederate General John Bell Hood at the Battle of Chickamauga. Of course, a Confederate flag always hung over the front door at Wyatt Hall.

In 1981, Margaret and Hubert were featured with a full-color picture in *The Tennesseans: A People and Their Land*, a book commissioned by Governor Lamar Alexander with photographs by Robin Hood and text written by Barry Parker. The Wyatts' friends were amused by the caption beneath the picture that described Margaret as "the most unreconstructed of Southerners" and a woman who never forgave the daughter of her kinsman, Jimmy Litton, for marrying a Yankee. When Robin and Barry stopped on impulse to see who lived in the antebellum house with a front gate made of horseshoes and a Confederate flag flying over the front door, they introduced themselves and explained to Margaret what they were doing. She invited them in, graciously served them biscuits and country ham, and regaled them with stories, one of which was that the only books anyone ever needed to read were the Bible and *Gone With The Wind*.

———◦◦◦◦———

For forty-five years, Hubert and Margaret attended harness races at The Red Mile track in Lexington. Their last trip was in 1981, not long before Hubert died. There and at other racetracks, Hubert and Margaret had met many fascinating people. Over the decades, they shipped horses by air to California and Europe and, in the days before air travel for horses was popular, they trucked horses to California and other states in huge vans. Because of their distinctive personalities and out-going natures, Margaret and Hubert were extremely well-known in the harness racing world. Many people said to them, "You are the two nicest people at the tracks."

Margaret's devoted husband Hubert died in 1982. The cause of death was an abdominal aneurysm. He also was diabetic. The loss of Hubert was a huge blow to Margaret. In 1984, a friend in Lexington called Margaret to say they all wanted her to come to a board meeting of the Stable of Memories organization. Margaret declined, and resigned from the board, having decided that, since Hubert had died, she was never going to the races again.

———◦◦◦◦———

After Hubert's death, Margaret continued to drive her enormous Cadillac wearing little old-fashioned glasses perched on her nose. She was not tall enough to look over the steering wheel. Consequently, when she forgot to put a pillow in her seat, she simply looked through the steering wheel. Anyone driving regularly between Wyatt Hall and Franklin knew to give her wide berth. When the time came, Margaret sold her beloved home, and disposed of her horseshoe collection, furniture, and other items that would not fit in the much smaller home to which she moved. Before moving, she and her good friends Evan Lloyd and Margaret Adamson of Shelbyville went to the condominium and carefully measured every nook and cranny to make sure Margaret could move as much furniture and memorabilia as possible. Her new address was Number Twelve Winston Court Condominiums, located on a bluff overlooking the Harpeth River at the end of Fourth Avenue South. Having planned the move carefully, Margaret was able to take with her an enormous number of horse-related items and other collectibles. Her visitors, including her Russell, McGaw, and Early nieces and nephews and their children, had to be careful where they sat when they visited their vivacious and generous kinswoman, whom they called "Sister." Of course, the doorknocker was still a horseshoe.

One day in the 1990s, the director at the Carter House brought Rick Warwick, Williamson County historian, by Mrs. Wyatt's condominium to meet Mrs. Wyatt. Before being introduced, Margaret asked Rick where he was from. When he said, "East Tennessee," she called him "a damn Yankee."

After a number of relatively good years, in which Margaret's health slowly declined, she reached the point where she needed to either have someone to stay with her or move to an assisted living facility. Margaret, who cherished her independence, did not want anyone living in the condominium with her. Her nieces, Kay Beasley and Margaret Ross, told her the best alternative was to move to NHC Healthcare, a division of National Health Care, on Fairgrounds Avenue in Franklin. Reluctantly, Sister packed her suitcase and made the move.

A premier hat designer in Nashville, who had, over the years, made many hats for Margaret, knew she was emotionally down and brought her a hat after the move. It was a navy straw hat covered with white flowers and Margaret loved it nearly as much as she hated the nursing home. She wore it when she walked down the halls. She also made it clear she wanted to return home, telling Kay and Margaret that she'd been kidnapped and imprisoned. One day, Sister told Kay that she saw a horse outside her window. Kay thought it must have been a dream, but who knows? In time, Margaret, who had little in common with most of the residents, primarily because she was much sharper mentally than they were, did go home, where she had round-the-clock help. When Margaret died in 2001, Kay Beasley called my wife and said, "Sister left instructions for her casket to be covered with a Confederate flag that had flown at Wyatt Hall. What am I going to do?" Irene said, "This is what Margaret wanted. You have to do it. Everyone will know she requested it." So Margaret was buried with the Confederate flag draped over her coffin. She was buried next to Hubert in Franklin's Mount Hope Cemetery. The only problem with their plot was that it was next to the plot of a family named North. I hope Margaret knew he was a Franklin boy.

Notes

CHAPTER TWO: Sarah Ophelia Colley Cannon

1. Minnie Pearl with Joan Dew, *Minnie Pearl, An Autobiography* (New York: Simon and Schuster, 1980), 13–14.

2. Ibid., 61–63.

3. Ibid., 87.

4. Ibid., 88.

5. Ibid., 121–22.

6. Ibid.

7. Ibid., 91, 136.

8. Minnie Pearl never employed top professional writers to turn out good material for her, as they were hard to find and very expensive. Conversation, Lillian Burns with the author, 12 December 2009.

9. *Minnie Pearl, An Autobiography*, 16.

10. Ibid., 23.

11. Nelson C. Andrews, "My Life," copy in the collection of the author.

12. *Minnie Pearl, An Autobiography*, 201-02.

13. Http://www.countrymusichalloffame.org, Inductees, Minnie Pearl.

14. *Minnie Pearl, An Autobiography*, 225–26.

15. Http://www.sarahcannon.com, The Sarah Cannon Cancer Center.

16. Ridley Wills II, *Tennessee Governors at Home*, (Franklin, Tenn.: Hillsboro Press, 1999), 84.

17. Mrs. Winfield Dunn's written reminiscences, 23 June 1998.

18. Conversation, Jo Doubleday with the author, 6 October 2009.

19. Conversation, Mary Ann Denney with the author, 28 September 2009.

20. Interview, Governor Ned Ray McWherter with the author, 24 September 1998.

21. Conversation, Kathryn Whitehead with the author, 24 September 2009.

22. Ibid.

23. Interview, Martha Sundquist with the author, 30 November 1998.

24. *Minnie Pearl, An Autobiography*, 240.

25. Http://www.sarahcannon.com, The Sarah Cannon Cancer Center.

Chapter Three: Neil Cargile Jr.

1. Bill Woolsey, "Backyard Aviator," *The Nashville Tennessean Magazine*, 13 June 1948.

2. E. Thomas Wood, "Stories of Neil," *Nashville Life*, December/January 1996.

3. Conversation, J. Bransford "Jake" Wallace with the author, April 2009.

4. Bill Woolsey, "Backyard Aviator."

5. Conversation, Thomas M. Trabue Jr. with the author, 4 July 2009.

6. Conversation, Franklin Jarman with the author, 24 July 2009.

7. Ibid.

8. Bill Woolsey, "Backyard Aviator."

9. Conversation, Julian Scruggs with the author, 17 March 2009.

10. Conversation, Mary Ann Stallings Maddin with the author, 22 March 2009.

11. 1954 *Commodore.*

12. Conversation, Franklin Jarman with the author, 24 July 2009.

13. Conversation, John Bransford Jr. with the author, 25 July 2009.

14. When Neil flew Connie out to Sikeston to see the house he had rented near his office and across the railroad tracks from the better part of town, Connie cried. She quickly found a nicer apartment on the "right" side of the railroad tracks.

15. Conversation, Edward G. Nelson with the author, March 2009.

16. John Berendt, "High-Heel Neil," *The New Yorker*, 16 January 1995.

17. Conversation, Ernest "Willie" Hardison Jr. with the author, 9 May 2009.

18. Conversation, Anne Byrn Roberts with the author, 20 July 2009.

19. John Berendt, "High-Heel Neil."

20. Ibid.

21. Ibid.

22. E. Thomas Wood, "A Nashville Life: Stories of Neil"

23. Conversation, Lynn May with the author, 13 March 2009.

24. Conversation, Martin S. Brown with the author, 14 May 2009.

25. *The Tennessean*, 3 August 1995; *Nashville Banner*, 3 August 1995.

26. *Nashville Banner*, 3 August 1995; John Berendt, "High-Heel Neil."

27. Maureen O'Sullivan, "Palm Beach Style: There Are No Rules," *Palm Beach Daily News*, 23 May 1993.

28. John Berendt, "High-Heel Neil."

29. Ibid.

30. Apparently, Neil did not always adhere to his practice of not going to the Belle Meade Country Club in drag.

31. John Berendt, "High-Heel Neil."

32. Ibid.

33. Ibid.

34. Ibid.

35. Conversation, John S. Bransford Jr. with the author, 25 July 2009.

36. Conversation, John Seigenthaler with the author, 25 February 2009.

37. "Socialite Neil Cargile Jr. dies of malaria," *The Tennessean*, 3 August 1995.

38. Ibid.

39. Ibid.

CHAPTER FOUR: Dudley Clark Fort Sr.

1. Conversation, Carole Minton Nelson with the author, 24 March 2009.

2. Letter, Dr. R. E. Fort to Dr. B. F. Finney, Vice Chancellor, University of the South, 9 September 1931.

3. In 1936, Dr. Fort received an honorary degree from the University of the South.

4. University of the South transcript 1932-33 for D.C. Fort, Archives, DuPont Library, University of the South.

5. Conversation, Arthur Godfrey Fort II with the author, 23 September 2009.

6. Dudley Fort was the first member of a National Life founding family to go on a debit in Akron, Ohio. The author, Ridley Wills II, was the second. Ridley worked on a debit in the Akron South office in 1960.

7. *The Shield News*, 1935.

8. Dudley C. Fort vertical file, archives, Jessie Ball DuPont Library, University of the South.

9. "Pink Coats," *The Atlanta Constitution*, 9 January 1957.

10. Kay Beasley, "Fort One of WWII's Unsung Heroines," *Nashville Banner*, 25 May 1988.

11. Dudley C. Fort vertical file, archives, Jessie Ball DuPont Library, University of the South.

12. Conversation, Arthur G. Fort II with the author, 23 September 2009.

13. "Dudley Clark Fort, 82, Dies in Belle Meade," *Herald Chronicle*, 21 November 1994.

14. Conversation, Margaret Sloan with the author, 22 March 2009.

15. Dudley C. Fort verticle file, archives, Jessie Ball DuPont Library, University of the South.

16. In addition to the gift from Dudley and Pearl, his sister-in-law Chloe Fort; his brother Rufus Fort Jr.; and Mrs. Ernest Hardison contributed to the stained glass window.

17. *Chattanooga News-Free Press*, 28 August 1963.

18. "Uncle Dudley's Spirit of '76," *The Nashville Tennessean*, 6 July 1966.

19. Conversation, Arthur G. Fort II with the author, 23 September 2009.

20. Dudley C. Fort file, archives, DuPont Library, University of the South.

21. Conversation, Edward G. Nelson with the author, 24 March 2009.

22. Conversation, Willie Gibbons with the author, 2 August 2009.

23. Conversation, Thomas N. Bainbridge with the author, 21 September 2009.

24. Pearl was at the Franklin County Health Care Center because her son, Dudley C. Fort Jr., was practicing medicine there and could conveniently check on her.

25. "Fort Scholarship Established Through Charitable Trusts," Sewanee Financial Planner, June 1993.

Chapter Five: Mildred Joy Cowan Gulbenk

1. Conversation, author with Anne Cowan (Mrs. Byrd) Cain, 13 January 2010.

2. Conversation, Anne Cowan Cain, 13 January 2010.

3. Conversation, Lynn (Mrs. Jack) May with the author, 21 September 2009.

4. Conversation, Betty Cook Sanders with the author, 2 December 2009.

5. Conversation, Larry Ray with the author, 10 October 2009.

6. Ibid.

7. Conversation, Eugenia (Mrs. Ben S.) Moore with the author, 9 October 2009.

8. Conversation, Eugenia Moore with the author, 9 October 2009.

9. Conversation, Betty Cook Sanders with the author, 2 December 2009.

10. Conversation, Roupen Gulbenk with the author, 2 October 2009.

CHAPTER SIX: Elizabeth Patton "Betsy" Howe

1. "Howe Rites Set For Wednesday," *Nashville Banner*, 13 July 1937.

2. Jackie Sharborough, "Smart, Cynical, Philosophical and Witty— She's All These and More," *The Nashville Tennessean*, 16 October 1960.

3. Conversation, Margaret Howe (Mrs. John) Sloan with the author, 22 March 2009.

4. Conversation, Jean Ewing (Mrs. Jimmy) Love with the author, 12 April 2009.

5. "Makes Debut At Brillant Reception," *The Nashville Tennessean*, 28 January 1934.

6. "Dinner Dance at 'Acklen' Given for Miss Anne Howe," *Nashville Banner*, 17 January 1936.

7. "Howe Rites Set for Wednesday," *Nashville Banner*, 13 July 1937.

8. "Mrs. John Howe Dies; Rites Today," *The Nashville Tennessean*, 22 July 1950.

9. Conversation, Harry Ransom with the author, 14 April 2009.

10. When Dr. Pilcher died prematurely in 1949 at age forty-five, neurological surgery lost one of its most promising and active minds.

11. Conversation, Margaret Howe (Mrs. John) Sloan with the author, 22 March 2009.

12. Warren Duzak, "Longtime Nashvillian Ann Howe Billings dies," *The Tennessean*, 22 December 2003.

13. Davidson County Death Notice, *The Tennessean*, 18 September 2007.

14. Conversation, Harry Ransom with the author, 14 April 2009.

15. E-mail, Robert L. Howe to the author, 5 April 2009.

16. Conversation, Harry Ransom with the author, 14 April, 2009.

17. Conversation, Bill Cammack with the author, 9 April, 2009.

18. Conversation, Margaret Howe Sloan, with the author, 22 March 2009.

19. Jackie Sharborough, "Smart, Cynical, Philosophical and Witty— She's All These and More," *The Nashville Tennessean*, 16 October 1960.

20. Ibid.

21. Ibid.

22. Conversation, Ellen More with the author, 7 July 2009.

23. Conversation, John Hardcastle with the author, 27 March 2009.

24. *The Nashville Tennessean*, 16 October 1960.

25. Ibid.

26. Conversation, Coleman Harwell with the author, 20 March 2009.

27. Conversation, Dr. Frederic T. Billings III with the author, 24 October 2009.

28. Conversation, Shade Murray with the author, 2 October 2009.

29. Conversation, Ann Street with the author, after Betsy's death.

30. E-mail from Ophelia and George C. Paine II to the author, 2 October 2009.

31. Conversation, Harry Ransom with the author, 14 April 2009.

32. Ophelia Paine, who was there, thought it was one of the best funeral services she had ever attended.

CHAPTER SEVEN: Andrew Lytle

1. Andrew Lytle, "Recollection and Reflection," *Mountain Voices: The Centennial History of the Monteagle Sunday School Assembly* (MSSA, 1982), 311.

2. Mark Lucas, *The Southern Vision of Andrew Lytle* (Louisiana State University Press, 1986), 3.

3. Andrew Lytle won Guggenheim awards in 1940, 1941 and 1960. Wilson, *World Authors*: 1950-1970, 893.

4. Deborah Kelley Henderson, *Robertson County's Heritage of Homes* (Nashville: Williams Printing Co., 1979), 46–47.

5. Lytle, *A Wake for the Living* (New York; Crown Publishers Inc., 1975), 161–62.

6. H.W. Wilson, *World Authors*: 1950–1970, 892.

7. Wilson, *World Authors*: 1950–1970, 893.

8. Note, Brad Gioia to the author, 10 August 2009.

9. E-mail, Pamela Lytle to the author, March 9, 2010.

10. Jon Meacham, "A Modest Case for a Burkean Boomlet," *Newsweek*, 1 June 2009.

11. Andrew and Edna Lytle's third daughter, Katherine Anne Lytle Liggett, died in December 1984 in Pensacola, Fla. *Nashville Banner*, 24 December 1984.

12. E-mail, Pamela Lytle to the author.

CHAPTER EIGHT: Dan May

1. Joseph L. "Jack" May, *A Confetti of Papers* (Nashville: privately published, 2008), 129–30.

2. "Dan May Dies; Had Metro Role," *Nashville Banner*, 17 December 1982.

3. May, *A Confetti of Papers*, 18.

4. William May Stern, *There's an Old Southern Saying . . . The Wit and Wisdom of Dan May* (New York: Crabby Keys Press, 1993), 125.

5. Ibid., 7.

6. May, *A Confetti of Papers*, 358.

7. Amy Lynch, *Service Above Self: A History of Nashville Rotary* (Rotary Club of Nashville, 1995), 129.

8. Ibid., 170.

9. Ibid., 115.

10. Ibid., 117.

11. Conversation, author with George H. Cate, Jr., 21 August 2009.

12. Stern, *There's an Old Southern Saying . . . the Wit and Wisdom of Dan May*, 15, 114.

13. Ibid., 15–18, 46–47

14. Ibid., 9.

Chapter Nine: Harvey Pride Jr.

1. "Pride-Dantzler Marriage Took Place This Morning in New Orleans," *Nashville Banner*, 5 January 1927.

2. Conversation, author with Trilby Elliston Williams, 11 April 2009.

3. Ibid.

4. Ibid.

5. Ibid.

6. Conversation, author with Lillias Burns, 11 December 2009.

7. Ibid.

8. Conversation, author with Trilby Elliston Williams, 11 April 2009.

9. Conversation, author with Eugenia (Mrs. Ben) Moore, April 2009.

10. Conversation, author with Craig Kelley (Mrs. Kenneth) Adkisson, April 2009.

11. Conversation, author with Trilby Williams, 11 April, 2009.

12. Conversation, author with Dan and Gene Pride, 4 July, 2009,

13. Reminiscences of George and Barbara Wilkins, 8 September 2009.

14. Conversation, author with Trilby Williams, 11 April 2009.

15. Ibid.

16. Conversation, author with Phillys (Mrs. Julian) Scruggs, 1 September 2009.

17. Conversation, author with Trilby Williams, 11 April 2009.

18. Ibid.

19. Ibid.

20. Conversation, author with Phillys Scruggs, 1 September 2009.

21. Harvey named his horse "Eran" for his mother, Eran Dantzler Pride.

22. "Fox Hunters Morn Loss of Two Fellow Riders," *Nashville Banner*, 3 January 1984.

23. Conversation, author with Ann Harwell (Mrs. Charles) Wells, July 2009.

24. Ibid.

25. Conversation, author with Dan and Gene Pride, 4 July 2009.

26. Conversation, author with Trilby Williams, 11 April 2009.

27. Jackie Burke, "Foxhunters Mourn Loss of Two Fellow Riders," *Nashville Banner*, 3 January 1984.

CHAPTER TEN: Frederick Tupper Saussy III

1. Bill Pryor, "Renaissance Man on The Run," *Nashville Life*, April/May 1996.

2. Reminiscence of Jeanie (Mrs. William) Cammack, September 2009.

3. John Branston, "Doing His Time: Tupper Saussy Tells His Tale," *Nashville Scene*, 14 May 1988.

4. Lola had a half-sister, Jeanie Hecker Cammack.

5. Alan Bostick, "Remember Tupper Saussy?" *The Tennessean*, 24 April 1989.

6. Bill Pryor, "Renaissance Man on the Run."

7. John Branston, "Doing His Time."

8. *The Tennessean*, 15 November 1997.

9. Nashville Symphony Orchestra Program, 13-14 January 1969, Tupper Saussy file, Archives, DuPont Library, University of the South.

10. *Nashville Banner*, 18 March 1986.

11. Bill Pryor, "Renaissance Man on the Run."

12. John Branston, "Doing His Time."

13. Bill Pryor, "Renaissance Man on the Run."

14. Ibid.

15. Ibid.

16. *The Tennessean*, 12 February 1975.

17. *Nashville Banner*, 17 September 1975.

18. *Nashville Scene*, 14 May 1998.

19. "The Gimmes: Taxmen are the Villains," *The Tennessean*, 13 August 1978.

20. Bill Pryor, "Renaissance Man on the Run."

21. Conversation, Bill Cammack with the author, 1 June 2009.

22. *Nashville Banner*, 4 December 1978.

23. Ann Betts, "Tupper Saussy Traveled from Belle Meade to Prison," *The Tennessean*, 3 March 1985.

24. *The Tennessean*, 12 July 1979.

25. *Cheekwood Mirror*, September 1979.

26. Bill Pryor, "Renaissance Man on the Run."

27. Alan Bostick, "Remember Tupper Saussy?"

28. *The Tennessean*, 24 September 1981.

29. Bill Pryor, "Renaissance Man on the Run."

30. Ibid.

31. "Federal Courthouse Incident Leads to Contempt Charges," *The Enterprise* (Winchester, Tenn.), 30 January 1985.

32. "Contempt Sentence Cut in Saussy Case," *The Enterprise*, 20 March 1985.

33. Ann Betts, "Saussy Pledges to Continue Tax Fight," *Nashville Banner*, 6 May 1985.

34. "1,000 in Freedom Organizations Planning to Gather Here May 2," *Chattanooga Free Press*, 23 February 1985.

35. Ann Betts, "Saussy Pledges To Continue Tax Fight."

36. *The Tennessean*, 6 May 1985.

37. "Attorney Says Saussy Knew His Filing Illegal," *Nashville Banner*, 30 May 1985.

38. Bill Pryor, "Renaissance Man on the Run."

39. "Saussy Gets Sentence on Income Tax Charge," *Nashville Banner*, undated.

40. John Branston, "Doing His Time."

41. "Tax Protestor Flees Sentence, Claiming Prison Won't Take Him," *The Atlanta Journal* and *The Atlanta Constitution*, 8 November 1987.

42. *The Tennessean*, 15 November 1997.

43. Bill Pryor, "Renaissance Man on the Run."

44. Mark Zabriskie, "On Playwright's Struggle," *Nashville Banner*, 18 March 1986.

45. Ibid.

46. "Tax Protestor Flees Sentence," *The Atlanta Journal* and *The Atlanta Constitution*.

47. *Nashville Banner*, 17 October 1986.

48. E-mail, Susan Binkley to the author, 25 March 2009.

49. Letter to the editor, *The Tennessean*, 18 November 1987.

50. *The Tennessean*, 24 April 1989.

51. Ibid.

52. John Branston, "Doing His Time."

53. Ibid.

54. Ibid.

55. Ibid.

56. Lola's second husband was Joe Francis of Nashville. They moved to Park Avenue in New York City. There, Lola opened a shop that sold Appalachian art and handmade quilts. Later she and Francis divorced. Lola's third husband was John French. By 1996, they were living in Key West. Bill Pryor, "Renaissance Man on the Run."

57. Bill Pryor, "Renaissance Man on The Run."

58. Ibid.

59. John Branston, "Doing His Time."

60. While living in Santa Monica, Tupper learned that his younger brother, William R. "Bill" Saussy died in Marathon, Florida, on 22 February 2001. Bill was only fifty-six. *Sewanee Messenger*, 1 March 2001.

61. Haun Saussy, "Tupper Saussy 1936-2007," personal reflections, 23 March 2007.

62. Ibid.

CHAPTER ELEVEN: Margaret Lindsley Warden

1. I did not include endnotes on this chapter as a majority of the stories came from Margaret's autobiography, *Life Has Been Very Kind to Me.*

CHAPTER TWELVE: Ellen Stokes More Wemyss

1. "Query Club," *The Tennessean*, 15 September 1988.

2. Walter Stokes Jr., "Hillsboro Pike and Something Personal," delivered to the Tennessee Historical Society, 13 October 1964.

3. "At 100, Gallatin Civic Leader Still Going Strong," *Nashville Banner*, 8 February 1995.

4. In 1988, the artwork was included in an exhibit of paintings of distinctive women of Tennessee at the Parthenon.

5. "At 100," *Nashville Banner,* 8 February 1995.

6. Hillsboro Pike became a free pike to the county line in 1901 when Davidson County bought the pike from its owners.

7. "Recollections by Ellen Wemyss," from a tape in the Nashville Public Library, edited by Ann Wells.

8. Louise Davis, *The Tennessean,* 15 June 1986.

9. Nancy Watkins, "Trail Blazer," *Nashville Women*, December 1997.

10. "Area Women Recall First Vote of 1920," *The Tennessean*, 19 August 1995.

11. In December 2008, Agnes and Livingfield More Jr. attended the dedication of "The E. L. More Memorial Bridge" over the Conecuh River at River Falls, Alabama; *Nashville Banner*, "Livingfield More Claimed by Death," February 9, 1934.

12. E-mail to the author from G. Sidney Waits, Covington County, Alabama, historian, 5 August 2009; letter from Livingfield More Jr. to the author, 19 January 2010.

13. E-mail from G. Sidney Waits, 12 July 2009; Nancy Watkins, "Trail Blazer."

14. This gift resulted in a lawsuit, Wemyss vs. Commissioners, in the Federal Court that Mr. Wemyss lost. The Supreme Court ruled for the IRS, and Congress later passed a landmark law based on the case.

15. "At 100," *Nashville Banner*; 8 February 1995. "William H. Wemyss, Genesco Cofounder, Dies in Gallatin," *The Nashville Tennessean*, 20 March 1973.

16. Thomas K. Connor, "Living With Antiques," copy in Mrs. William Wemyss file, Nashville Room, Nashville Public Library.

17. In 1922, Ellen, Cornelia Keeble, and Katherine Craig went to Atlanta to ask the Atlanta Junior League to sponsor a Junior League in Nashville. The Atlanta league did so and the Nashville Junior League soon became a reality. "Recollections by Ellen Wemyss, 1980," from a tape in the Nashville Public Library.

18. "Granny Happy Sets Tea Table at Fairvue," *Nashville Banner*, 8 June 1977.

19. Ibid.

20. "At 100," *Nashville Banner,* 8 February 1995.

21. When Ellen was seven years old, the Tennessee Central Railroad came through the Stokes farm on Hillsboro Pike, effectively cutting the farm in two equal parts.

22. *The Nashville Tennessean*, 17 November 1957.

23. Ibid.

24. "Mrs. Wemyss Wins Garden Club Award," *Nashville Banner*, 24 April 1968.

25. "William H. Wemyss, Genesco Cofounder Dies in Gallatin," *The Nashville Tennessean*, 20 March 1973.

26. "The Mistress of Fairview Celebrates a Century," *Nashville Life*, February/March 1995.

27. Letter, Livingfield More Jr. to the author, 29 December 2009.

28. "Historic Site," *The Tennessean*, 2 June 1981.

29. "At 100," *Nashville Banner,* 8 February 1995.

30. Conversation, author with Walter Durham, 7 July 2009.

31. E-mail, William G. "Bill" Coke to the author, 26 July 2009.

32. Letter, Livingfield More Jr. to the author, 29 December 2009.

33. Ibid., "At 100," *Nashville Banner*, 8 February 1995.

34. E-mail from Fletch (Mrs. William) Coke to the author, 21 July 2009.

35. Conversation, author with Anna (Mrs. Walter) Durham, 7 July 2009.

36. Ibid.

37. "Querry Club," *The Tennessean*, 15 September 1988.

38. Nancy Watkins, "Trail Blazer."

39. Ellen Wemyss's grandchildren gave her the nickname "Granny Happy."

40. "The Mistress of Fairview Celebrates a Century," *Nashville Life*.

41. E-mail from Ann Wells to the author, 14 July 2009.

42. *The News* (Gallatin), 29 February 1996.

43. Jennifer Peebles, "Lifelong Activist Fought for the Past," *The Tennessean*, 5 June 2001.

44. Nancy Watkins, "Trailblazer," *Nashville Woman.*

45. In 2000, Mrs. Wemyss's stepchildren sold Fairvue and its 400 acres to developers. Construction began on an upscale housing development on the property; she was allowed a life estate. Earlier, she had talked to the author about giving Fairvue to the National Trust for Historic Preservation, but this never materialized.

46. Jennifer Peebles, "Lifelong Activist Fought for the Past."

CHAPTER THIRTEEN: Margaret Early Wyatt

1. I did not include endnotes on this chapter as most of the stories in the chapter came from Margaret's autobiography, *Nothing Happens By Chance*, published in 1992.

Index